MW01075563

The Pet Loss Companion
Healing Advice from Family
Therapists Who Lead Pet Loss Groups

Judy McNamara

In memory of Lione Mae
7/9/2008 - 3/26/2017

You Will Never Be
Forgotten.

Ken Dolan-Del Vecchio & Nancy Saxton-Lopez

Copyright © 2013 Ken Dolan-Del Vecchio
Nancy Saxton-Lopez
All rights reserved.

ISBN: 1484918266
ISBN-13: 9781484918265
Library of Congress Control Number: 2013909131
CreateSpace Independent Publishing Platform,
North Charleston, South Carolina

Cover art by Tim Garrett

Cover photograph by David Patiño

Praise for *The Pet Loss Companion*

Everyone who's ever loved an animal companion will find wisdom and solace in this book. The authors share stories drawn from decades of experience leading pet loss groups and practicing family therapy. Their recommendations for taking care of yourself and loved ones during the rough spots of grief will answer all of your important questions and help you feel well-supported. I highly recommend *The Pet Loss Companion* for companion animal lovers like me.

— Ed Sayres, President & CEO of the ASPCA®

The Pet Loss Companion is a wonderfully reassuring book for anyone who cares about pets. It is a loving book, full of personal and practical details about how to care for oneself after loss. The authors are sensitive pet-lovers, empathic and engaging in this moving and meaningful book.

— Monica McGoldrick, MSW, Ph.D. (h.c.), Director, Multicultural Family Institute, and author of *You Can Go Home Again*

If you have ever lost a beloved pet and have wondered if your feelings are normal, this book is a must read for you. Ken and Nancy, in this single book, have captured the emotional roller coaster that most people experience during the end stages of the life of their pet. In addition there are helpful insights into their world as bereavement counselors and how they have helped their patients deal with the experiences of death. I have practiced Veterinary Medicine for over 30 years and have finally found a book that can be given to my grieving owners after such a trauma.

— Anthony Miele, DVM, CEO, Veterinary Asset Management, Inc.

What a gift Ken and Nancy's book is to those of us who have cherished and lost a pet companion. They get it, and as such, gently and skillfully help to ease the treacherous journey that loss is. This gem explores the terrain of loss and grief and the vast love that surrounds the experience. Readers will be warmed, saddened, and delighted by the examples and tools that are provided to ease the necessary grief process. The experience of reading this little book leaves me feeling much gratitude for my pet companions and these authors who so beautifully convey the huge role they play in our lives.

— Lynn Parker, Ph.D., LCSW, Professor, Graduate School of Social Work, University of Denver

St. Hubert's Animal Welfare Center is proud to offer free pet loss support as part of its programmatic efforts, with Nancy Saxton-Lopez at the helm for over 20 years. Together Ken and Nancy continue to provide this valuable service at our center twice monthly and they've expanded their reach by sharing their professional training and direct pet loss counseling expertise with the completion of *The Pet Loss Companion*. Their compassion for both pets and the people who love them is palpable in this concise, easy-to-read guide which offers understanding, solace, and hope to anyone struggling with the loss of a cherished animal companion, no matter the circumstances. The loss of a companion animal is a unique, yet not unique, grieving process not always well understood by others. This book connects and thereby supports people at a time of what can be isolating grief, providing a life raft or light to navigate the process. It's also a helpful tool—whether as a gift or for personal awareness—for those looking for some guidance in supporting family and friends coping with pet loss.

— Heather Cammisa, President & CEO, St. Hubert's Animal Welfare Center, Madison, New Jersey

To all who grieve,
may your heartache be brief,
your love, everlasting.
- KDDV

To my best friends, confidants, and loves: the dogs
of my childhood,
who taught me how to trust, love, and give.
- NSL

Contents

Foreword

Pets matter to you and me. They are family. We commit ourselves to their care, we talk with them, we love them, and we grieve when we lose them. I have related to animal companions in this way for as long as I can remember.

Although few other children my age lived nearby in the rural upstate New York community of my youth, I never lacked friends. I spent hours with our family's dogs—hiking, running, and after we got tired, laying in the grass watching the sky. I still cherish those memories, sometimes closing my eyes and calling them to mind following a particularly challenging therapy session and at other times for meditation.

The adults in our house, my parents and grandparents, were kind to our dogs, some of whom my father and grandfather valued as hunting partners. They even invited the dogs inside on snowy winter days to toast themselves by the kitchen woodstove. However, my elders never used the word *love* to describe their feelings for an animal, unless maybe they were talking about the chicken on their dinner plate.

I, on the other hand, loved each of our many dogs. My brother and I counted nine during our years at home. I grieved when they died the same as I would for any other loved one. This set me apart, a reality driven home one afternoon when I was eleven years old. I watched helplessly as my best friend, a brown and white beagle mix named Skippy, was hit by a car after I got off the school bus. Distraught, I almost knocked over my grandfather as I raced back toward the house. In between my sobs I told him what happened.

"Oh hell, Nance, we'll get you another dog!"

Grandpa's words hit hard, leaving me doubled over and crying such that I struggled to breathe. I was alone in my grief.

That was one of the moments that inspired my interest in pet loss counseling. My journey includes launching the first pet loss support group in New Jersey. Ed Sayres, then the president of St. Hubert's Giralda (an animal welfare and education organization) in Madison, New Jersey, and now president of the American Society for the Prevention of Cruelty to Animals (ASPCA), provided the opportunity to get started. Through Ed I met Carolyn Carpenter, an interfaith minister, and together we hosted our first pet loss group at St. Hubert's on April 3, 1990—kismet, for the first dog who had become mine during my adult years, Tashi, had died on April 3, 1989. The group has been meeting ever since.

When Carolyn moved to Colorado in 2001, I invited my friend Ken Dolan-Del Vecchio to take her place. Ken and I had met while working as therapists at a hospital in Morristown, New Jersey. With me based in the emergency room and Ken mostly on the inpatient behavioral health ward, our paths crossed when emergency room patients were admitted for a hospital stay. We got to know one another through chats at the edges of our work with incoming patients and their families.

Sharing news about our own families, including my expanding pack of pugs and cockatiels and Ken's menagerie, where cats seemed the companion animal of choice at the time and the family horse was boarded nearby, we recognized one another as kindred spirits. To be sure, we also talked about our human family members, our spouses and children—my only child, Elisa, now twenty, is six months older than Ken's only child, Erik. If truth be told, however, it was our love for animals that made us friends.

Pet loss support, while a passionate interest for both Ken and me, does not make a therapist's living. I work as a partner in a behavioral health management consulting firm. I also practice as a psychotherapist, helping families and individuals through all manner of life challenges.

Ken works as vice president, health and wellness, at a multi-national corporation. His team delivers programs and services that support behavioral health and build leadership skills. On the side, Ken speaks to conferences and community groups on intimate partner violence and diversity affirmation.

I was thrilled when Ken asked me to join him in writing this much-needed book. Ken had previously coauthored a family therapy textbook and written a book of his own that helps couples heal their relationships. He showed me his manuscript for *The Pet Loss Companion* and said, "I'd like our book to be short (because people often find it hard to concentrate when they're grieving), easy to read, personal, and full of practical advice."

After reading what he shared, I told Ken, "I think it's wonderful: what readers need is mostly here already, plus it's laid out simply and with a personal tone." From there, we set about further refining the content and adding my thoughts and experiences, being careful not to unnecessarily expand the book's length.

The result, the book you hold in your hands, comes to you mostly in Ken's voice, with my thoughts and recommendations blended in. We share our combined experience supporting people through the loss of their animal companions and offer *The Pet Loss Companion* with great hope that it helps you heal.

— Nancy Saxton-Lopez 1/27/2013

Preface

A Unique Loss

The loss that compelled you to open this book has much to teach you about love, life, and the value of your most important relationships. What you learn may be among the most significant gifts that your deceased pet leaves you. We urge you to hold your grief in this spirit.

When we lose a pet, we lose a relationship unlike any other. And unfortunately, we must expect to lose them as nature gives most companion animal species a life span much shorter than our own. We may lose the first family member to greet us every morning as we get out of bed and every evening when we return home. We may lose the one friend from whom we hide nothing. He or she may have heard our most secret desires, seen us at our very best and worst, and loved us steadfastly throughout. We lose a soul who shared our life journey up close and personal. Many of us lose one of the most meaningful relationships we have ever known.

In the immediate aftermath of this unique loss, we too frequently confront an excruciating paradox—family members and friends will oftentimes tell us not to feel troubled by our friend's death. "She was only an animal." "Why don't you just get another one?"

People say such things despite the fact that many of us love our pets the way we love our children. We provide for their every need. This often includes bodily care that brings to the relationship a kind of intimacy known elsewhere only between parents and infants. In return for all that we do, our animal companions give their complete devotion. Kindness offered and kindness returned: a unique equation in the formula of love. Unique, because the devotion we receive from our pets never suffers the shortcomings of human love, such as cynicism, manipulation, and unfaithfulness. Instead, their unconditional love remains constant. In addition to this special kind of love, our relationship with a pet provides other gifts found nowhere else. If we pay close attention, animals can teach us how to live in the present moment more effectively than any human being can.

Instead of devaluing your grief over the loss of this important relationship as others may advise, we encourage you to hold dear the sorrow that follows the loss of your pet. We urge you to move through this challenging time placing trust in your thoughts and feelings. Embrace them wholly for they will light up your path of healing and teach you important things about what matters most in life.

Chapter 1

Introduction: The Circle of Love and Grief

For a combined total of more than three decades, Nancy and I have led support groups for people whose dogs, cats, rabbits, birds, horses, and fish—yes, even fish—have died. We've been trusted with stories of love and grief, each one helping us better understand what it means to be a human being, deepening our appreciation for life and the relationships we cherish. Twenty-five years ago, when I was a young therapist, a wise woman told me that we inevitably pay for our love with grief— "inevitably" because all relationships end. She also promised that love proves to be worth its cost every time. We've seen the truth in her words told countless times by people after losing their companion animals. We wrote this book to share what we've learned.

Companion animals draw our attention in a unique way. Not long ago while on vacation, my spouse, our two best friends, and I ambled toward our docked cruise ship along a busy street in Ireland's seaport town of Cobh. We marveled at the pastels of yellow, pink, and green row houses lining our steep descent, the grey stone cathedral, and the water directly ahead that mirrored the sky's rainy blue and filled the serpentine contours from harbor to horizon. The sights and sounds of this foreign place captivated us.

Suddenly, a small bouncing fluff of white grabbed our attention in a way that pushed everything else aside. Ten paces ahead a young Irishman's West Highland white terrier had jumped up from his "sit and stay." One after another, people smiled and dodged the ten-week-old puppy. Many of us couldn't resist stopping. Smiling broadly, the young man told us he was teaching his pup street manners. After the rest of us stroked the puppy's head, my friend, David, scooped her up and cooed, "Aren't you adorable!" He held her against his face. Smitten.

What captivated us in that flash of bouncing white fuzz? I believe we're drawn to companion animals by their absolute innocence. These are beings who present themselves exactly as they truly are—no pretense, vanity, or self-consciousness. Nobody would doubt the sincerity of my four-pound, long-haired Chihuahua, Isabel, as she bounces, yips, and wiggles her curled-over plume of a tail upon my arrival home each evening. Like other companion animals, she radiates an "other worldly" measure of honesty. Indeed, our companion animals bridge us to the world of fields, open sky, forests, and rivers. They bring us close to nature in a way that many people find healing. The relationship we enjoy with a West Highland white terrier, one-of-a-kind (mixed-breed) kitten, Mini Rex rabbit, parakeet, or other companion animal enriches our lives in ways that no human-to-human bond can. We learn to become more generous, compassionate, open, caring, and even more responsible, through our relationships with animal companions.

When I was a six-year-old boy, my parents moved to Coventry, Rhode Island. Our new next-door-neighbors, the Gerbers, included Pete, my age and soon-to-be best friend, and his older brother, John. While my parents were not yet willing to take on the responsibility of a dog (that would take two years of begging from my two older brothers and me), the Gerbers, on the other hand, were rich in animal companions. Their family included Fifi, a tiny, delicate, grey and white cat; Tom, an enormous orange tabby; and a seventy-pound, mostly reddish-brown and black, long-haired, dog of indeterminate breed named Zeke. I remember the three of them as if 1966 were yesterday, and though each of these animal friends touched me, it was Zeke who grabbed my little-boy heart.

Zeke relentlessly nudged Pete and me when he wanted attention, which was most of the time we shared his company. He was always up for a game of fetch with a stick, ball, or Frisbee, and no day of fishing would have been complete without Zeke's look-out-he's-gonna-shake-all-over-you, soggy-dog smell company. His black velveteen muzzle fronted a broad retriever face, and he considered us pups through soft dark eyes, the eyes of a canine sage.

In those days before the wisdom of leash laws and neutering, Zeke periodically disappeared for two or three days at a time. He would return home damp, his fur fringed with pond muck. We'd guess that he had swum across Johnson's Pond, the largest body of water in our area and the pond on whose banks we enjoyed our best days of fishing. I can still feel the sense of mystery that surrounded our "what ifs" when our friend disappeared: was Zeke really a spy sent on secret missions and living with Pete's family just his cover? Today, of course, I imagine that our wandering lothario was making his rounds, visiting a string of female friends.

When Pete and I were seven, Zeke disappeared forever. I can still visit the pain when we realized we would never see or touch Zeke again. In my mind's eye I see Pete's mother leading her two sons, along with my brothers and me, in a reading of goodbye letters, followed by a trip to the local soft-serve ice cream shop. On the drive home we celebrated our friend's life and marked his passing with stories to remember him by, more tears, and drippy ice cream cones.

Zeke lives in my heart today. He's joined there by Shaggy, the dog of my begging boyhood who became a member of my own family and died while I was away at college; Pinky, my first rabbit; and the many other companion animals who have shared my life. Each brought me joy, each taught me something about the nature of love, and each left me struggling through the journey of grief. For all the sorrow that these losses brought, however, I've never regretted sharing my life with any one of these souls. As that wise woman promised so many years ago, love proved worth its cost every time.

So let us begin our journey of love, grief, and discovery.

This book offers simple truths about the nature of grief and suggestions on how best to care for yourself through its duration. The chapters that follow will also help you manage the sometimes challenging responses of family members, friends, and coworkers; prepare for the fact that people grieve differently; navigate the feelings that accompany a decision to euthanize; decide what to do with your companion's remains; decide if and when to adopt another pet; decide whether or not it makes sense to consult a behavioral health professional; and help the children in your life with their grief.

Respecting the way that grief often limits attention spans, we've strived to deliver much helpful information in a minimum of text. Each chapter concludes with a list of summary points to help you remember what's most important. The book's small size also makes it easy to carry as a ready source of support.

Because stories help us gain understanding, you'll find many in the pages that follow. We share stories from people who have participated in our pet loss support groups, friends, members of our families, and our own life experiences. We have altered details to screen identities and, in some cases, drawn more than one real-life account into a composite.

We bring you these stories because each teaches something important about the journey of grief, the enduring value of love despite inevitable loss, and the special place that animal companions claim within our lives as a whole. This last point, I should explain, finds its origin in our profession of family therapy. You will see that we look at grief from a perspective that considers its effects upon relationships with family members, friends, your workplace, and community.

If you have recently lost an animal companion, we ask you to revisit the beginning of this chapter. Remember, your deep sadness reflects the intensity of your love for your departed friend. Your friend lived richly as the recipient of your great love. And while we convey the following suggestion with some apprehension as we know it may mean little at present, we hope you allow yourself to imagine a moment sometime in the future. In that moment some time from now, you'll know that to have loved so fully means you have received one of the most special gifts that life grants us.

Please be gentle with yourself. Remember that you deserve special care during this challenging time and resolve to treat yourself accordingly.

Chapter 2

Is My Grief Normal?

Many people worry that the pain of their grief exceeds what's normal and healthy. Nancy and I can assure you that unless you become so incapacitated that for a period of several days in a row you can't take care of the basic necessities like bathing, dressing, and feeding yourself, you can consider your grief perfectly normal. Unfortunately, however, even normal grief can make you feel like everything, including your sanity, is falling apart. This chapter describes some of the experiences that fall under the heading "normal grief."

Feeling shocked, numb, and forgetful

Grief often begins with a numbness that distorts your senses and ability to think. I work as vice president, health and wellness, for a multinational corporation. My job gives me responsibility for a number of programs related to behavioral and organizational health. On the morning of September 11, 2001, I drove from my home in New Jersey to one of the company's largest sites, located in Dresher, Pennsylvania. There I planned to deliver a seminar for a conference of business leaders on the skills necessary for managing people during stressful times. (We could not have known how important that set of skills would become.)

Upon my arrival in Dresher, the conference's coordinators asked me to join them in a classroom next to the main auditorium. We viewed a television report that included video of the South Tower of the World Trade Center collapsing. After some discussion, we decided that I would be the one to break the news to the eighty or so participants next door.

Moments later I stood before the conference attendees in the auditorium, microphone in hand, poised to inform them of the unfolding tragedy.

While I had seen the images of the collapsing tower—television news reports had already replayed this footage a number of times—I said to the group something like, "Both of the towers have been badly damaged and are burning." Immediately after saying those words, I remember thinking, "Why didn't you say that a tower had collapsed? You saw it collapse but the words wouldn't come out. You saw it collapse but you don't believe it."

My thinking and perception weren't working as usual. I remember time moving slowly. I felt detached. I remember feeling almost as though I was watching myself speak to the group rather than feeling fully present in the usual way. These kinds of changes often accompany new grief.

As you hold your pet while he draws his last breath or when you discover her body stretched lifeless on her favorite cushion, time may fall into slow motion. Your own body may suddenly feel impossibly heavy. You may feel strangely disconnected from the thoughts, motions, and sounds of the moment. Many people describe this as feeling like they're "on autopilot."

Later, they may not even recall all of what happened. One woman told her group, "My mother said that after discovering my cat's body in the living room I combed and brushed her before wrapping her in one of the family's best towels for the ride to the vet's office. I didn't remember any of that. I was looking for that towel yesterday and my mother reminded me that I'd left it at the vet's office. I was dumbfounded when she told me about how I prepared her body."

Disbelief and disconnection may numb you in this way when the loss first hits, and every now and then, thereafter, as well.

A chaotic mix of feelings

Grief can bring a jumble of mixed feelings. Despair, anger, guilt—and sometimes even happiness—rise and fall, often in rapid succession and for no obvious reason. As you ride this roller-coaster you may find that one day—or indeed one minute—you'll cry your eyes out, the next you'll feel angry at yourself or at your pet's veterinarian, and then all of a sudden you'll laugh at a memory that popped up seemingly from nowhere. Parents scratch their heads watching their young children bounce from tearful sobs of "I miss Fido!" to smiling, focused play. People of all ages go through rapid shifts in mood when grieving.

Moving through this kaleidoscope of emotions leads many people to question their sanity. Rest assured that this strange mess of feelings, while terribly uncomfortable and at times frightening, fits well within the description of normal grief. You are not losing your mind.

Problems with basic body functions, including sleeping and eating

You may find yourself sleeping too much or too little. You may drag yourself out of bed and pull yourself together so you can get ready for work and care for others who depend upon you. You might have been dead asleep for ten hours but you feel like you haven't slept at all, or you may have tossed and turned without ever really falling asleep. Sometimes you've got your usual appetite for food; other times you may overeat and, still other times, have no appetite at all. And if all that isn't hard enough, grief can also make you hurt in the same places where other stresses tend to strike you. For some people, that means suffering more headaches. Others may get stomach aches or back pain.

Memory and concentration lapses

Many people find that their ability to think clearly, concentrate, and remember deserts them. You may ask the same questions over and over again. When given answers, you listen with all the attention you can muster but retain absolutely nothing. These memory lapses can complicate everything from grocery shopping to the work you do to make your living.

Guilt

Some questions you repeat not because you can't concentrate or because memory fails you, but rather because you can't escape the flood of guilt and second-guessing that washes over you.

"Why didn't I notice that she was dehydrated?"

"How could I have been away from home when it happened?"

"I wonder if he'd still be alive today if I'd gotten him to a specialist earlier instead of trusting our vet's original diagnosis."

Nancy and I hear comments like these at every pet loss group.

No matter what heroic measures you may have taken, grief can still make you question whether you did enough. We've heard people tell of driving twenty-two miles for their arthritic German shepherd's aqua-treadmill physical therapy sessions twice weekly for many months, and cooking special meals for their cat all of her life due to chronic kidney problems, and having an animal chiropractor and masseur work on their elderly rabbit. These same people tearfully describe their regrets at not having done more. Guilt may not become a major feature of your grief. But if it does, you will be far from alone.

New losses reawaken earlier ones

After any major loss, including the death of an animal companion, many people find previous losses coming to mind. When my dog, Lily, died five years ago I found myself revisiting the deaths of my father and grandmother, both of whom had left this world decades earlier, as well as the deaths of previous animal companions.

Remembering these earlier losses didn't add to my pain. Instead, the memories helped me place Lily's life and death within the landscape of all the loving relationships I've known.

Please try to keep a positive perspective if you find yourself revisiting past losses. Remember, grief eventually heals us. You can aid the healing by trying whenever possible to claim a positive understanding of the experiences through which grief brings you.

Mysterious visits from your lost pet

Many people see, smell, and experience the touch of their departed friend. In one particularly memorable account, a family told the story of their boxer, Patches, who at one time had a favorite toy that rarely left his mouth. Patches carried his miniature football so constantly for a time that it seemed a part of him. He greeted family members and guests displaying his ball but never giving it up to share, his stubby tail wagging all the while. The toy eventually disappeared into the yard and was all but forgotten.

One afternoon shortly after Patches' death the family's two children, aged twelve and thirteen, settled into their homework at the kitchen table. Familiar sounds of scratching and whining at the back door startled them. They opened the door and there on the stoop lay the long lost football, damp and dirty as though it had been retrieved from some muddy hiding place.

Patches' guardian told the other members of the group, "A six-foot picket fence surrounds our back yard, we lock the gates from the inside, and this muddy toy that we hadn't seen for months lay in the center of the stoop. We can find no alternative explanation beyond the most obvious and mysterious one. The kids took it as a sign that he's okay and we're content to follow their lead."

These kinds of "visits" occur regularly. Stories of this sort expand the limits of what many of us have been taught to believe possible. Nancy and I have come to regard them as evidence of the miraculous power of love.

Expect inconsistent progress

"Normal grief" includes all of the above, and it rarely progresses in an orderly fashion. You may find that you've encountered sad moments during the past couple of days but not the rush of tears that seemed to strike every few hours before then. You step into a grocery store where *Somewhere over the Rainbow* or another sentimental song plays and the tears arrive with such force that you fear all progress has been lost.

During moments like that it can help to remember that most people move through grief in a one-step-forward, two-steps-back, three-steps-forward, one-step-back fashion. You will eventually find longer periods of calm reflection and the ability to focus more on matters other than your loss, but the journey can be a strange one. For most of us, it doesn't feel like an orderly progression from point A to point B. Instead it feels more like rafting down the Colorado River, complete with disorienting rapids and deadening doldrums, as well as some welcome periods of calm progress.

Nancy and I remind those who attend our groups that grief is a process, not an event. In the beginning you may feel that you have lost a piece of yourself, indeed you may feel a "black hole" within your soul.   Eventually, however, that void will fill with positive memories. Our assurance of this may mean little as you read these words now, because grief requires time.

Grief takes time

Simply stated, grief takes whatever amount of time it takes, and that varies tremendously. Many people find themselves less encumbered by grief after a year has passed. Experiencing the world without their lost friend across seasonal changes, major holidays, important family anniversaries, and other annual milestones helps them come to terms with the loss. For some people grief persists well beyond the first anniversary of their companion's death. Others note their grief lessening after only a few weeks or months.

Several years back I read a study showing that most Americans believe there's something wrong with a person who still expresses feelings of sadness three weeks or more after the death of a loved one. The study revealed how poorly informed many people are when it comes to loss and grief. Unfortunately, mainstream culture continues to avoid a reasoned approach to death and dying, leaving many of us unprepared to deal with this unavoidable aspect of life.

Grief changes us

Finally, we'd like you to know that eventually you will grow stronger as a result of your grief. Grief will bring you to a new place that's different from where you were before your loss. You may grow more resilient, flexible, and appreciative. Some people find that grief increases their capacity for gratitude. Many people increase their understanding of the complexity of life. Ultimately, grief brings wisdom, a point that we'll expand upon later.

Key points

1. Normal grief can make you question your sanity. It helps to keep in mind that unless you're not able to manage the basic necessities, like bathing, dressing, and feeding yourself, for a period of several consecutive days, then your grief is perfectly normal.
2. Normal grief often disturbs patterns of sleep, appetite, energy, attention, memory, and concentration.
3. Grief can move you through a swirl of rapidly changing states of mind, including shock, despair, anger, confusion, acceptance, reflection, and joy. Most people feel better sometimes and worse at others without a steady forward progression.
4. Each loss brings grief with a time frame all its own.

Chapter 3

People Grieve Differently

There may be as many ways to grieve as people who lose loved ones. Let's imagine that you've shed only a few tears since your pet died. While you haven't felt the need to cry, the image of her lifeless form, like a photograph that you can't forget, intrudes upon your thoughts several times each day. You can't stop wrestling with the same questions. *Did she know how much I loved her? Did I really show her? Did I do everything I could to make her happy?* You find yourself in a solemn frame of mind much of the time.

Your spouse, on the other hand, who shared in the discovery of your pet's body and who convulsed into red-faced wailing, anguish such as you'd never seen before, howling that went on for more than twenty minutes before coming to a sudden halt, has not shed a tear since and seems not the least disturbed.

Neither your experience nor your spouse's qualifies as more correct or healthy or sane or intelligent or effective. They simply differ. While we will suggest reasons for the differences, the most important point to remember: *many different ways of grieving are normal and healthy.*

Please don't listen to anyone who tells you otherwise. *This includes you.* Too many of us hear an inner voice that judges. So if you wonder whether the way you grieve meets quality standards, replace that question with this more helpful one: *What can I do to take even better care of myself during this difficult time?* We'll explore this important question and its answers later on.

We grieve differently because each of us has different life experiences and temperaments. These shape how we do everything, including how we grieve. The more we come to accept this fact, the less troubled we find ourselves when we bump into our differences. Instead of getting upset, we can pay attention with an open heart and an open mind. Approaching different grieving styles with an attitude of openness will allow you to learn important things about yourself and the people with whom you share your life.

The life experiences that influence grieving style include gender, cultural heritage, history of loss and grief, the kind of relationship we had with our deceased companion, the circumstances of their death, the level of support we receive from others, the balance of stresses present in our lives at the time of our loss, as well as our spirituality and beliefs about death.

Gender

Despite the loosening of widely-held gender rules during the past several decades, a development that has helped both men and women become more complete human beings, we still can't discount gender entirely when it comes to patterns of grief. Most women communicate their thoughts and feelings more readily than most men. The old rule that "big boys don't cry" still grips many of us. Consequently, women tend to express their grief more freely and men tend to express their grief in a more reserved fashion. Of course, this does not hold true for *all* women and *all* men but the pattern persists.

Cultural heritage

Ethnicity shapes the way we understand and interact with the world, including the way we grieve. The Italian side of my family favors the open demonstration of most feelings, including the deep sadness and moments of anger that come with grief. The English and Swedish sides of my family lean toward more stoic expression. I usually show my Nordic side, preferring to think through (some therapist friends of mine would say 'intellectualize') my feelings rather than demonstrate them with abandon. Your ethnicity (or collection of ethnicities as the case may be) likely influences the way you grieve as well.

History of loss and grief

While each loss brings unique challenges, previous experiences with loss and grief affect the way we respond. Those who have never lost a pet, human family member, or close friend, may feel completely unprepared for the anguish that follows their pet's death. Even if you have not suffered a death in the family, you have probably survived other significant losses, perhaps including lay-offs at work or the end of dating relationships and cherished friendships. Remembering the way you felt after these losses may provide a frame of reference that makes the emotional ups and downs of your current grief at least a bit more familiar and, therefore, more manageable.

Some people have endured the loss of several pets and family members. As a result, they may feel prepared to manage their grief. The distress they experience has a familiar feel and they recall how in the past their pain diminished over time. Other times, however, people who have experienced many losses find themselves nonetheless surprised by the extraordinary intensity of their present grief. They learn that, while grief follows a somewhat predictable pattern, each loss stands unique among all others and brings its own measure of emotion.

As was mentioned earlier, new losses often call previous ones to mind. These resurrections can prove challenging. When we reflect upon particularly traumatic losses, such as the death by violence of a pet or a human family member, such recollections can make our current grief more complex.

Our relationship with the deceased pet

The loss of our Chihuahua, Lily, deeply affected me. Weighing only two-and-a-half pounds, Lily was a tiny wisp of a dog. She had long, fine golden hair and a golden heart as well. Lily always wanted to be held. She followed her people about, spinning in circles and crouching into her "play with me" bow whenever someone even hinted that they may bend down to greet her. Like many dogs of her small stature, she behaved warily around children, however. She seemed to fear, perhaps wisely, that a child might handle her tiny frame less carefully than would an adult.

My son, Erik, who was eight at the time Lily came into our lives, noted her wariness and favored her more robust cousin, Jack, who joined our family at the same time. Erik and Jack, an oversized Chihuahua who weighs twelve-pounds and resembles a miniature dingo, became best buddies. Erik never failed to treat Lily with kindness but she always kept her distance.

Erik was saddened by Lily's death but he also said, "Lily never warmed up to me so I never felt that close to her." While Lily's death tore at my heart, Erik's different relationship with her lessened the impact for him. Similarly, you may find that members of your family, having had different relationships with your lost pet, grieve differently as a result.

No matter how many companion animals you have and how much you love each of them, there may be one or two who touch your heart like no others. Something about your pet's personality and your own may fit together unusually well. Or perhaps the special bond grew while sharing particularly eventful times. Nancy will always remember her first pug, Tashi, with special fondness. Nancy and Tashi lived through seven changes in residence, Nancy's divorce, several new job opportunities, and Nancy's remarriage. After Tashi died, Nancy's grief confined her to bed for several days. Nancy says that Tashi will always be her "first lady."

We regularly speak with people who provided extraordinary care during their pet's final illness. They may have carried their dog outside whenever she needed to move her bowels, having lost the ability to walk the distance required; or several times each day they may have dressed a wound that wouldn't heal properly; or they may have administered fluids under their pet's skin daily as a treatment for kidney failure. Providing such intimate care builds extraordinary closeness, and this tends to intensify the grief you experience.

The circumstances of your pet's death

The circumstances of a companion animal's death can play a role in shaping your grief. Nearly all conscientious pet guardians struggle with some degree of guilt. *I should have noticed the (insert here a sign or symptom that would be impossible for any human being to actually notice) and taken her to the vet earlier.*

Some guardians have difficulty forgiving themselves because they happened to be traveling, asleep, or at work when their friend died. Other people faced the trauma of being present yet unable to change the course of fate when an accident claimed their pet's life, such as when a pet chokes to death. At the far end of the continuum lie situations in which the pet's guardian made an error that *actually did* contribute or lead directly to their pet's death: a dog asphyxiates after being forgotten in the car on a summer day, a cat finds her way into a crawl space and eats rat poison, a ferret breaks into the chinchilla or guinea pig's pen and does what comes naturally to predators, in a moment of inattention by his or her guardian the dog's expandable leash allows her off the sidewalk and into the path of an oncoming vehicle.

Whatever the circumstances of your friend's death, you deserve to remind yourself that human beings have limitations. We can't foresee the future in order to make sure we're in the right place at the right time, and we can't fix every twist of fate that places our friend in harm's way, and we regularly make unfortunate mistakes. Finally, we deserve to remind ourselves that we never intentionally cause harm to our loved ones.

Support from others

Few things help more during stressful times, grief as a prime example, than the support of other people. Knowing that others care makes the burden of grief easier to bear. As the following example illustrates, support can make the difference between trauma and manageable loss.

Sam and his fiancée, Jill, both in their early twenties, attended a pet loss meeting a few days after the gruesome death of Trotsky, their four-year-old Siberian Husky. While enjoying an evening jog with the couple, Trotsky yanked toward an approaching commuter train and managed to slip out of his collar. The couple watched helplessly as the train struck Trotsky, killing him instantly.

Sam and Jill recovered Trotsky's shattered body. They called a friend, who met them with his car. Together, the three young people buried Trotsky under a tree that had been one of his favorite marking places.

After Jill and Sam told the story, including horrific details regarding the state of Trotsky's remains, others commented on the strength with which these "kids" had faced the horror of their friend's death. Jill and Sam nodded their heads and clasped their hands together tightly. Through their tears they told the group that this experience taught them about their ability to pull together and help one another during a crisis. The support they gave one another and the validation they received from the group helped enormously. Had they not enjoyed such wonderful support, but instead faced their loss alone, their grief may have proceeded with greater difficulty.

Pet loss groups provide a concentrated dose of social support. Meeting with others who also grieve, hearing their stories, and sharing strengths can boost one's healing greatly.

The balance of stresses in our life

It can be challenging enough to lose your pet, but if your companion animal dies at a time when you're experiencing additional personal hardship, such as the recent loss of your job, the need for a major home repair, or an elderly parent requiring hospitalization, you face an even more difficult situation. On the other hand, your healing from grief will be strengthened if no other extraordinary changes have happened recently, you enjoy a fine state of health, exercise regularly, consistently eat a well-balanced diet, and love your chosen work.

Beliefs about death and spirituality

Whether you belong to an organized religion, practice a more individualized approach to spirituality, or consider yourself an atheist, spirituality shapes the way you grieve. People who believe in an afterlife often find comfort in the expectation that they will reunite with their deceased pet following their own death. Many such people, on the other hand, feel troubled because their faith also teaches that animals do not have souls and, therefore, can't enter heaven.

Some people feel their pet's spirit near them immediately following their friend's death. Their spirituality includes a belief that death introduces the soul to another dimension, one not far removed from our own. People who hold this kind of faith report feeling close to their deceased pet in a new way.

Atheists may accept their loss as final and claim the process of grief as the path necessary to come to terms emotionally with the end of this important relationship.

Temperament

All of our life experiences combine to shape our temperament, which can also be called personality style. Our temperaments, in turn, shape our life experiences by affecting the ways that we understand and respond to events, including the loss of a pet. As an example, a young man who I spoke with recently came from a family that always included at least two dogs and two cats.

"In my family, pets were well-loved and treated like royalty. When they died, we held a funeral in our back yard rock garden. My parents still live in the house where I grew up. There must be twenty-five rocks in that garden that mark a pet's final resting place. My parents treat death as just another part of life. They've taken every one of our pet's deaths in stride. I guess I've got a similar temperament when it comes to loss. I get really sad, but never loud, shrieking sad. I stay calm and just kind of take the loss in stride as a part of life."

As with life experiences, temperaments vary considerably. People known for their loud, boisterous demeanors may show their grief differently from people like the young man mentioned above, who tends toward a quiet, thoughtful manner. The former, sometimes called extroverts, draw energy and comfort from crowds. "The more the merrier" fits their style. They may enjoy sharing the details of their lives and losses, even with people with whom they have just become acquainted.

Other people, sometimes labeled introverts, feel drained by the presence of a group. They may guard their privacy and seek comfort in solitude. These people may do most of their grieving alone.

Some people love the language of feelings. They describe what goes on in their inner worlds with a precision that seems effortless. For them, sadness comes in many hues and it helps to talk about them all. Other people struggle to find words for their emotions and feel less inclined to discuss matters of the heart. When they're grieving, these people may enjoy a concerned friend's silent company more than the exchange of words.

People who tend toward worry and regret, those prone to reviewing life events through a lens of "would have, should have, could have," move through their grief differently, often facing a more difficult time than those who rarely second-guess.

Some people favor writing, jogging, sparring with a punching bag, dancing, playing a musical instrument, or creating art in the form of photography, collage, drawing, painting or crafting, over talking. They may heal their grief mostly through activity.

Finally, it helps to remember that none of us fit any one of these temperaments exclusively. Instead, most of us fit several, depending upon the circumstances. I have known men who will share their grief openly and with great feeling when in the company of their older brother or father, but will remain stoic otherwise. Personally, I work through many of my emotions without saying a word (except inside my head) while I jog and lift weights, but I also share my thoughts and feelings freely with family members and others who I have grown to trust. My temperament, like most everybody's, shifts depending upon where I am and who I'm with and what we're doing at the moment.

Negotiating differences honestly can bring great benefits

When members of couples pay attention to their differing responses without judging one another the information gained can turn potential conflict into increased closeness. George and Marge, a couple who I saw as clients in my family therapy practice, grieved very differently following the death of George's horse, Wizard. Their frank discussion of these differences opened new possibilities for their marriage.

Four weeks prior to our first meeting, Wizard, George's twenty-two-year-old Belgian Warmblood, the friend with whom George had spent the most time during the previous thirteen years, was euthanized. Wizard's death suddenly ended one of the most joyful periods of George's life.

Thirteen years prior, George had retired from a satisfying career as corporate counsel at a multinational pharmaceutical firm. Immediately thereafter, he dove into his equestrian dream. He purchased Wizard and the two began dressage training under the direction of one of New Jersey's most sought-after instructors. George spent nearly all of his time at the barn and equestrian events. In the evenings he read everything he could find on horse care, dressage, and equestrian culture.

Wizard was a stout bay fellow with a quiet temper who nuzzled every hand hoping for a carrot or apple. He moved like a dream under saddle. George and Marge agreed that a better friend and more committed dance partner would be hard to find.

Fine one day and gone the next, Wizard's death as the result of colic had stunned the couple.

Marge loved Wizard almost as much as did George, and she would miss him greatly. Within a week, however, it became evident that the loss left George and Marge in very different places emotionally. George, preoccupied with sadness and guilt, and missing the structure that training and caring for Wizard had provided, spent hours reviewing the last days of Wizard's life. He tormented himself with guilt over Wizard's death.

Marge, on the other hand, discovered herself feeling more relieved than sad. She wondered what she and George might do together during some of his newfound free time. She also found herself feeling angry with George about the depth of this grief because it prevented him from doing much besides moping. George's grief left Marge feeling alone.

Marge reflected on how her relationship with George had changed over the years. Wizard's death had reawakened memories of that time thirteen years past when he first entered their lives. His death had reawakened other losses, as loss so often does. For Marge it was the loss she had experienced following George's retirement that came to mind most of all.

Marge had supported George's career for decades, maintaining their household, nearly single-handedly raising three sons to adulthood, and playing the role of executive's wife and hostess. Having put aside her own aspirations for so long, Marge had looked forward to George's retirement with great anticipation. She envisioned a time when her desire for European travel and extended visits with their grandchildren, all of whom lived in other states, would finally rank high on the couple's priority list.

She had found herself sadly mistaken, however, after the momentous date arrived and George began filling his time with equestrian pursuits. If truth be told, Marge came to see Wizard not only as a good friend but also as an imposition on her marriage. Reviewing this history made Marge very sad.

Marge decided to share her thoughts and feelings with George. She told George that she could see how despondent he felt and that she felt some of the same sadness but other things as well. She told George about her reflection, following Wizard's death, on the time just before Wizard came into their lives, a time when she looked forward to seeing more of George. Marge told George that she didn't like that she was feeling angry regarding the way his grief made him unavailable. She felt a strong need to talk with him about this so they could work through the loss and their future plans in a way that met both her needs and his.

George listened carefully. He listened without judgment and without reacting. He liked Marge's suggestion that they seek a therapist's help sorting things out.

As the couple and I spoke, we acknowledged not only different grieving styles and different responses to this loss but also the need to negotiate more fairly. While Marge loved to ride, her passion for all things horses paled before George's single-minded zeal. Marge's passions included European travel and spending more time with the couple's sons and their families. Building closeness would require George to devote less time to riding and more time to activities of interest to both spouses. George committed to meeting this challenge.

This couple's differing responses to their companion animal's death could have driven them farther apart. Instead, because they approached their differences thoughtfully and without judgment, their relationship deepened in understanding and closeness.

In summary, each of us grieves differently. We can link these differences to varied personal experiences and personality styles. Considering your own personal experiences and temperament can help you gain a better understanding of what you and your loved ones are going through following the loss of a pet. This exploration can also help you let go of negative judgments and learn to respect differences. Finally, as we'll discuss in the next chapter, understanding your own unique grieving style can provide clues about how to care for yourself.

Key points

1. Expect that you and the people closest to you may respond differently to the loss of your companion.
2. Approach both similarities and differences with openness.
3. Listen to others whom you love and respect regarding how best to approach differences that you find challenging.
4. Don't allow differences to create a wedge in your relationships—talk with one another.

Chapter 4

How Will I Get Through This?

A pet's death can throw you into a whirlwind of emotions. The storm may rage, ebb, and flow so unpredictably that when your emotions eventually calm down, the realization that the worst has passed may take you by surprise. That happened to me after Lily died. Several months later, I came across two photos of Lily and our surviving Chihuahua, Jack, as tiny puppies. The pictures had been taken seven years earlier at the home where they were born in Catskill, New York, just moments before we put our new babies into their crate for the long drive home to New Jersey. As I looked at the photos, it occurred to me that I was smiling. At last I could remember Lily and smile. I felt the pull of sadness, too, and some tears came, but they were tears of gratitude for having had her in my life. My grief had done much of its work.

Grief will gradually turn your unbearable recent news into manageable older news, too. We promise. Your loss will become more familiar and tolerable. Unfortunately, much of what you face between now and then lies outside your control. You can't regulate the flow of your emotions, and you can't direct the ups and downs of your appetite, and you can't bring order to your periods of clarity and confusion. You can decide, however, many of the things that you will and won't do to take care of yourself, and these decisions can lessen your suffering.

Kindness always helps

While always a good thing, kindness becomes even more important at a time like this. First, let kindness guide how you talk to yourself. When you wake up in the morning thinking about what you may have done differently, better, or more of in order to save or prolong your pet's life—regrets like this plague many people— stop this train of thought in its tracks. Remind yourself that grief brings unreasonable second-guessing. Begin anew with a reality check about all that you did for your friend: you loved your pet, you did everything you could to make their life a good one, and you deserve to remember those things instead of berating yourself with a list of would-should-could-haves with no connection to reality.

And if you—out of the blue—start to cry on the way to work, instead of becoming frustrated, pull to the side of the road and turn off the engine. Allow yourself to cry. Welcome the emotion as evidence of how much you loved your friend. When you calm down, congratulate yourself for managing your grief with such respect for your own feelings.

When you find yourself doing things that feel awkward or embarrassing, instead of judging, respond with kindness and maybe even a bit of humor. Nancy and I have heard many people— adult men and women—confess that in order to get a solid night's sleep they have to hold their deceased pet's stuffed toy, leash, or collar. We can't tell you how many times we've heard people ask some variation of, "What kind of weirdo needs to hold a stuffed duck in order to get a night's sleep?"

A woman recently described how she and her elderly father faced devastating sadness after the death of their cocker spaniel. Two weeks later, they were to attend a cousin's birthday celebration, but being exhausted, they decided to pass up the event. Wanting badly to attend the same cousin's wedding several weeks later, the two decided to approach this event differently in order to take care of themselves.

"My dad and I didn't want to miss the wedding but we still felt pretty drained by our grief. We decided that we'd drive down to Philadelphia the day before the wedding and make a leisurely weekend of it. We drove down on Friday, we went to the wedding on Saturday without any of the time pressure we would have felt if we'd started out from New Jersey that morning, and we drove home without any urgency on Sunday. We did it this way because we really wanted to be kind to ourselves throughout the trip."

Responding to your own thoughts, feelings, and actions with kindness rather than impatience, embarrassment, disdain, or some other negative judgment will lessen your suffering.

Extend the same kindness when you deal with other people. You may feel tested by some of the comments coming your way, even from those who mean well. As we'll discuss further in Chapter Six, when people make suggestions like "maybe you should get another pet to take your mind off your grief," they may have the best of intentions. Try to extend the benefit of the doubt. Let them know that, while you appreciate their kind wishes, bringing another pet into your life will not help at present. (As we'll discuss later, there may also come times when people say things that do *not* arise from the best of intentions. In those circumstances, other strategies apply.)

Choose the people with whom you share wisely

If you're like most people, few things will help more than spending time with others who love and respect you. Sharing your grief can lessen the burden, and simply being with people who understand can help you feel better. But because many people do not relate to companion animals the way you, Nancy, and I do, it becomes important to choose carefully those with whom you share your thoughts and feelings. We've heard too many stories in which an outpouring of sadness was met with, "Geez, it was only an animal, get over it already." It shouldn't be this way, to be sure, but we don't want you to be next in line for that cruelty.

Even people with whom you have shared many other personal stories and received much understanding may respond with unexpected insensitivity when it comes to pet loss. Many people see animals as if they were non-living objects. Surprisingly, this even includes some people who have pets.

A friend's neighbor not too long ago told me that her five-year-old cat had suddenly taken to urinating outside her litter pan. "She's messed up my carpeting and I'm not happy about it." I advised her to have the cat seen by a veterinarian as that behavior often suggests a urinary tract infection. Several weeks later I ran into the same woman, again. I asked how her cat was doing. She said, "I had her put down—she was peeing all over the place and that got old real quick."

Like this woman, many people see pets as ornaments that exist solely for the amusement of people, rather than living beings, similar to you and me.

Unfortunately, you need to keep this in mind when sharing your grief. In particular, we caution you about doing so at work. Some people receive tremendous support from their coworkers, including heartfelt compassion during lunch and coffee break conversations, sympathy cards, and loving voicemail messages. Other people open up at work and receive everything from thinly veiled disdain to outright ridicule. We've even heard people say that telling their bosses about their grief over a lost pet hurt their performance appraisals and opportunities for advancement.

Sharing your grief with those who care for you and respect your feelings for pets can help tremendously. But you can't assume you'll receive the same degree of support from everyone. If uncertain, reveal your grief tentatively and gauge the response carefully. It may work better to simply wait until you're in the company of those you know you can trust.

Also, remember that some people may offer only time-limited support, becoming less understanding after a week or two. You have a right to grieve for as long as you need.

As we've mentioned before, attending a pet loss group can help. Gathering with other people who share similar experiences offers a unique opportunity for support and empowers participants to give one another validation and advice. A skillful facilitator enriches the discussion by shaping the conversation so everybody gains from it. An internet search or your veterinarian can help you locate the one that meets nearest you. The book's final chapter presents an example of the discussion that you can expect at a pet loss group.

Online support

Many people receive great support from their friends on social media. One colleague of mine noted that he and his adolescent children were deluged with heartfelt condolences after posting news of their dog's death on Facebook. All three remember the outpouring of support online as a great source of comfort.

Mind the basics of health

Grief, like any other form of stress, takes a lot out of you, so balance the stress of grief by doing everything you can to keep yourself as healthy as possible. Eating well, getting enough rest, and avoiding other sources of stress go a long way.

Of course, grief can undermine your best efforts. Low energy and decreased initiative can present serious challenges. Many people don't feel up to the task of food preparation and default to fast foods, so-called comfort foods like French fries, pizza, and other less-than-healthy processed food. Grief reduces some people's appetites and energy so much that they miss meals. Others go to a different extreme. They soothe themselves by binging on junk food or drinking too much alcohol (and in some cases using other substances as well). Eating healthy at a time like this can be hard, but the benefits prove so valuable that you owe it to yourself to make your very best effort.

It helps to plan ahead and accept assistance when it's offered. Allow others to shop and prepare food for you if they volunteer, and include on your shopping list fruits, vegetables, and other unprocessed foods. Eating well will help you weather the stress of grief.

Similar challenges apply when it comes to getting enough rest. Grief can wreak havoc here. Many people find relaxation tapes, stretching exercises, and herbal teas helpful as sleep aids. If insomnia strikes, it may help to remember that grief normally brings some difficulty sleeping and this will likely pass. Of course, if you lose a lot of sleep, it makes sense to consult with a health care professional.

Finally, because grief itself qualifies as major stress, it helps to avoid adding new sources of stress. This will not be the best time to start remodeling your kitchen, throw an event for fifty guests, or request new assignments at work. Paring down responsibilities and commitments for the time being makes better sense. A word of caution here: temperaments vary. One person's stress can be another's healthy distraction. For some people, a new project can actually alleviate stress because it channels their excess energy. Let self-knowledge guide you.

Keep moving

Winston Churchill has been credited with saying, "When you're going through hell, keep going." These words carry special meaning now. It helps to put one foot in front of the other and keep moving forward when every fiber of your being resists. While it may feel difficult on some mornings, you will always feel better after getting out of bed and completing your usual habit of showering, grooming, and dressing in preparation for the activities of the day.

And once you're up and moving, you may feel inspired to move right into your exercise program. Physical exercise boosts feelings of well-being and calm, lessens muscular tension, improves sleep, and brightens your mood. Stretching, yoga, and other meditative practices fit the temperaments of some people better than walking, jogging, cycling, or lifting weights. You can gain similar benefits whether you prefer the more active or meditative options. All of them boost resilience and lessen the suffering of grief.

If you don't already exercise regularly, you couldn't choose a better time to start. That may sound absurd given the current circumstances, but this chapter emphasizes ways you can help yourself when so much lies outside your control. Nancy and I are willing to take the risk of sounding ridiculous if what's written here may help you. The decision to move your body —even taking short walks as a start—lies squarely within your control, and it can only help.

Experiment with routines

The routines that give your life structure may become a mixed blessing.

On one hand, the familiarity of your daily schedule can provide reassurance and predictability. Let's say that every weekday your clock-radio goes off at 6:00 a.m. You shower and then make your customary breakfast of scrambled eggs, toast, and fruit before heading out the door for work at 7:15 a.m. Keeping this routine can assure you that life, though forever changed by the loss of your friend, goes on.

On the other hand, this same pattern may emphasize your pet's absence. Maybe your clock-radio wakes you up in the morning, but it was really your dog's insistent licking of your face or hand or foot, that got you up and moving with a smile. She always waited for you just outside the shower and no morning would have been complete without tossing her a slice of banana or a piece of cheese during breakfast. Finally, your most enjoyable activity each morning may have been your walk around the block, which gave your dog the opportunity to do her business and got you some fresh air to start your day.

Your morning routine in this case provides structure but also triggers many heartrending memories. If you don't feel like making changes, it may help to actively acknowledge each memory that brings sadness by saying a few words out loud "to" your lost pet: "[Your pet's name], thank you for being such a wonderful friend, for being there in the morning and making me smile. I'll never forget you." Saying these words out loud creates a ritual that can help express your feelings of sadness, acknowledge the change, and move you ahead with a less heavy heart. (As you'll see, Nancy and I value rituals highly. They help people by pulling meaning and feeling together within a brief but powerful experience.)

33

After trying this affirmation of the usual schedule, you may want to experiment with changes. Let's suppose that your current routine includes working out at a health club most evenings at 6:00 p.m. (there I go again with the exercise). You may decide to switch your schedule around so that you awaken earlier, perhaps 5:30 a.m. instead of your customary 6:00 a.m., and go to the gym first thing in the morning. Some people find that changing their schedule lessens their distress. Others find keeping the usual pattern more helpful. Experimentation will show what works best for you.

A similar kind of experimentation can help with many aspects of your daily routine. For example, some people feel the need to remove their deceased pet's food and water bowls, beds, toys, photos, and other reminders immediately following their death. If you fall within this group, please consider storing such items for a time rather than discarding them altogether so you'll still have them available should you change your mind. (If you eventually decide to part with them, please remember that most animal shelters will happily receive donations of pet supplies, including food and medication.)

It helps some people to rearrange furniture. Many people move their pet's favorite chair to a new location. One man got terribly sad whenever he sat in his favorite place on the couch because his cat had always curled up next to him. He ended up buying a new set of living room furniture.

We have met a number of people who recreate the routine of their dog or cat sleeping in or next to their bed by purchasing life-size stuffed animals and placing them where their pets used to sleep. Allow yourself to experiment. Both changing and preserving your memory-rich routines can ease your grief.

Your workplace

Many people take a brief absence from work after they lose their pet. The time away allows them to face the reality of loss and devote full attention to the beginning of their grief. The structure, activity, and distractions gained at work, however, can contribute to healing after the initial shock has passed. As with many other daily patterns, it makes sense to listen to your heart and do what feels right for you. In general, however, a fairly rapid return to work, as well as the other major activities of daily life, helps people heal.

Creativity can help

Writing, scrapbooking, photography, and other creative arts may help you express, reflect upon, share, and hold your thoughts and feelings. When expressed in ways different than the spoken word, you will experience emotions from fresh perspectives.

Some people keep a journal or write stories, poems, or songs. A farewell letter to your pet can help express your gratitude with clarity and precision. While it may be challenging to write, completing the letter can prove uniquely healing because you can re-read it any time thereafter and recall the words that best describe your feelings. Most people decide to save the letter in a special place.

Many people find solace in creating what they call altars or shrines. These range in complexity from a dresser's top corner reserved for your pet's collar and favorite toys to far more elaborate creations. One woman announced to her group that she had erected a "stone altar" within her living room dedicated to her pet's memory. While she did not offer details, she clearly took great comfort in this achievement.

Photography can help. Many people carry photos of their deceased pet with them at all times. Some create remembrance albums or scrapbooks featuring photos that capture the main events of the life shared with their pet. People often come to pet loss groups with their albums and sharing these always becomes a highlight of the meeting.

Other people paint, draw, or make collages and other forms of visual art. I have seen ceramics, jewelry, knitwear, tapestries and fiber art inspired by the artist's love for their deceased pet. In every case, both the creative endeavor and the end result contribute to healing.

Plan for special calendar dates

It can help to plan ahead for certain dates, including anniversaries, birthdays, and holidays. In the beginning, plan for milestone days, such as the day of the week when your pet died. For example, if you anticipate having difficult Mondays for the next several weeks because you had to euthanize your pet on a Monday, consider scheduling a visit on the next several Monday evenings with friends or family members who respect what you're going through. Remind them that your feelings may be particularly tender because of the "anniversary" that Mondays represent.

It can also help to plan a brief ritual for each day that holds special significance. Depending upon your temperament, you may or may not want to invite others to participate. Staying with the example mentioned above, you may plan to devote five minutes every Monday evening to remembering, by either saying out loud or writing in a journal, one of the lessons you learned from your deceased pet, or something about them that you'll always remember. Maybe, you'll simply spend those minutes silently recalling what it felt like to be in their company. As an example, I might write, say, or think to myself, "Reggie taught me that the people and pets who I love sometimes try my patience but that doesn't mean I love them any less." A ritual such as this can help you revisit your connection with your friend and thank them for a gift you'll cherish.

Establishing a definite time frame, in this case five minutes on Monday evenings, honors your pet because you know you're going to devote time exclusively to their memory. It also limits your distress because you've decided to confine your recollection to a specific number of minutes.

There are many pet loss websites that offer bereaved pet owners a place to post a memorial online or enter a chat room to speak with others. Such websites may prove especially helpful on days that hold particular relevance for you.

Holidays can bring special challenges. Here again it can help to plan for the occasion. One woman knew that her first Halloween without Bast, her enormous black cat, would prove especially sad because "Bast always helped me give out candy." After thinking long and hard, she decided to spend Halloween evening running a children's party at a local domestic violence shelter.

Many people experience anxiety with the *first* major holiday that follows the loss of their pet. For some, like the woman just mentioned, it makes sense to plan a celebration very different from usual. They may decide to spend the day traveling with a friend when in years past they spent the day at home entertaining family members. Other people may choose to preserve a holiday practice, such as hanging a Christmas stocking for their deceased pet over the fireplace mantle. It may be helpful to include a brief ritual to both honor your deceased friend and contain the time you devote to sadness. For example, you may find it healing to read a holiday card written to your pet and then place the card in a prominent location. Advance planning can help you observe anniversaries, holidays, and other special dates with a minimum of pain.

Spend Time in Nature

Whenever you intentionally carve out time from your busy schedule to stroll through a park, hike a woodland trail, or walk a quiet stretch of beach, you give yourself a valuable gift, one that brings special benefits when your heart has been torn by grief. In nature, you find yourself surrounded by circular stories of life and death. Brittle leaves from seasons past shield tender, green shoots as they reach skyward. The shells of creatures from long ago lie strewn along the seashore. A hermit crab, his residence a grey spiral bequeathed by a sea snail, crunches into a defensive huddle at your approach. As you look at the crab, imagine how many lives his home may have sheltered. Fresh air, bird songs, the rustling of leaves and the dappled sunlight cascading through them, the sights and sound of waves, water idling in a pond or tumbling down a rocky stream—all of these bring the soothing embrace of the natural world.

Visiting such settings, however briefly, brings comfort to many people. As you endure the emotions that follow the loss of your pet, the continuity evident in the natural world can bring a special kind of solace.

Key points

1. Caring for yourself requires planning and sometimes supreme acts of will, as grief can diminish your energy and motivation for action.
2. Trying new activities (daily routines, creative projects, and holiday plans) proves helpful for many people.
3. While you can't avoid grief, you can lessen your distress through thoughtful acts of self-care.

Chapter 5

Losing Your Pet Can Hurt More Than Losing Your Parent

Nancy and I often hear people say that the death of their pet stirs more intense grief than any previous loss, including the loss of a parent, grandparent, spouse, or sibling. People almost always say this in a hushed tone, as though they can hardly believe that they feel this way and are confessing to it. We reassure them by acknowledging how regularly this occurs. We hear this so frequently, in fact, that we'd like to take some time to talk about it here.

Intimacy and grief

Intimacy means emotional and physical closeness. We often develop extraordinarily intimate relationships with our companion animals. They live in our homes, they follow us from room to room, and they sometimes even snuggle up next to us for their night's sleep. While we do not speak one another's languages, most of us talk to our pets as freely as we talk to our human family members.

Many pet guardians feel they can read their pet's moods and sometimes even their specific desires. We know when our pets feel happy, excited, worried, frustrated, angry, frightened, curious, hungry, stuffed with food, under the weather, and in need of a place to empty their bowels or bladder. We may experience an almost telepathic degree of understanding.

In addition to this emotional closeness, many of us experience a degree of physical closeness with our pets that goes well beyond what we share with most of the people in our lives. We may bathe our pets, clip their nails, clean their ears, swab the gunk out from their eyes, comb and brush them. Depending upon the kind of pet, we may also need to clean some of their most private body parts, scrape out the muck from their feet, and brush or file their teeth.

The only parallel that comes to mind is the way parents care for their infants. In that case, however, care of the infant's body decreases over time, and the intuition that guides parents gets supplemented by the exchange of words as a baby moves past his or her first birthday. With our pets, however, intimate bodily care continues throughout their lives and, because we can never exchange words, our intuitive bond continues to grow.

As pets grow older, their need for care intensifies because later years often bring infirmities. We may find ourselves injecting fluids under our pet's skin every day to stave off kidney shutdown. We may be required to cajole our pet into swallowing pills or liquid medication necessary for managing heart disease or cancer or digestive problems. Some people assist their pets in moving about because their legs or hips or back no longer function properly. Getting these things done requires us to touch, hold, and carefully manipulate our pet's body every day. For most of us, handling another living being in this caring way with such regularity brings them close to our hearts.

The extraordinary emotional and physical closeness that we enjoy with our pets creates a rare degree of intimacy. Also, our relationship with a pet stands alone in its simplicity. We never suffer unfaithfulness, manipulation, or major conflict. There were no arguments, periods of estrangements, and dramatic reconciliations with your deceased pet. The relationship was consistent, predictable, and reliable to a degree rarely achieved in our relationships with other people.

When you lose a connection of such intimacy and consistency, it's no wonder that the resulting grief may hurt even more than the loss of a parent or other human family member. We often live at some distance from our parents, siblings, and extended family. While we may love them greatly, our family members may not play a role within our daily lives. Instead, we may speak with them on the phone and visit them periodically. When we lose them, we lose somebody of immense importance but their death doesn't change the membership in our household and our daily routine. We don't lose someone who we have talked to and touched with our hands every day.

Extraordinary bonds

While an intimate bond exists to a greater or lesser extent between most pets and their guardians, sometimes the connection rises to an even higher level. Many pet guardians bond with one or more of their pets in a manner that feels extraordinary. My spouse and I once had a cat named Phoebe. Small in stature, solid black, with slightly curved tips to her ears and large golden eyes, Phoebe was a Bombay who we adopted from a cat shelter in Manhattan. From the moment we first greeted one another I felt as though I had known her for all of eternity, and I assumed, from the way she took to me, that the feeling was mutual. Phoebe shared our New York City apartment, as did Reginald, our tan and white cat. Those two cats followed us about our home. It seemed their life's mission was to maintain physical contact at all times with one or the other of us. While I loved them both dearly, something about the connection between Phoebe and me was different from all of my previous bonds with pets.

When Phoebe died a piece of me went along with her. Nothing had prepared me for the depth of sadness that followed her passing. Until that time, I had no idea that losing an animal friend could hurt so much.

When a person tells me that the death of a pet has torn their heart open like no previous loss, when somebody confesses that they grieve for their animal companion with a despair deeper than what they felt when their father or mother died, I think of Phoebe.

While I cannot account for this phenomenon with any greater clarity, I can attest to having experienced it twice (I have such a connection today with my dog, Isabel), and I have witnessed it countless times in the stories of friends, family members, and participants in pet loss groups. When we lose a pet with whom we enjoyed this kind of relationship, our grief can feel like nothing we've experienced previously.

When your pet's death marks the end of an era

Sometimes the loss of a pet results in extraordinary grief because they helped us through an extraordinarily difficult time in our lives or because the pet's death marks the "end of an era" in our own lives. A friend recently described how she adopted her dog right after separating from her husband, who had been abusive to her throughout their ten years of marriage. After her dog died, she suffered extraordinary grief.

"Jellyroll had seen me through my divorce and getting a whole new life started in a new town. She was the one I cried to and she always licked my tears and made me laugh. I adopted her from the shelter because I needed a friend and she turned out to be the best friend I could have wished for. When she died, it was the end of an era in my life. I thought back on everything I'd accomplished during those ten years. I'd gotten remarried, this time to my soul mate, I had a solid job that I enjoyed, and I owed so much to the way she stood by me and loved me."

When a pet has seen us through major life changes, our grief may be surprisingly powerful. In a sense, we're grieving not only for our deceased friend but also for all the changes that happened during the time we shared. The loss of our friend powerfully reawakens all the losses endured together.

A similar kind of intensity often results when a deceased pet was shared with a deceased or ex spouse, or when a pet was bequeathed by a late parent or child. Your pet's death in this case may powerfully re-energize feelings associated with the loss of your human family member. As we've mentioned elsewhere in this book, new losses reawaken previous ones. We can be almost assured that this will happen when such a direct link exists between the loss of a pet and the previous loss of a family member.

You have no reason to feel guilty

If your grief over a lost pet feels more extreme that the grief you felt after your mother died, you're likely to experience guilt. Nancy and I can't imagine anybody feeling otherwise. Even so, we'll argue that you should do everything possible to talk yourself out of that guilt. After all, you don't have control over how you feel. None of us does. Our feelings have a life of their own and they don't always make sense—far from it. Just look at the intensity of feelings that some people tie to sports teams. I know people whose entire week can be dampened when the New York Giants football team loses. That doesn't make any sense at all (at least to me). Still, it happens all the time.

We've described some factors that can contribute to the loss of a pet feeling worse than the loss of a parent, sibling, or other important human being. Nowhere within these descriptions—please note well—did you find any suggestion that you loved or valued your human family members less than your pet. Instead, we described the unique degree of physical and emotional closeness between pets and their guardians, the special bond that exists between some animals and their human guardians, and the way a pet's death can close an important era in one's life. All of these may contribute to the exceptional pain you experience. Finally, please remember that if you grieve more for your pet than you did for your parent or another beloved human being, this doesn't mean that you willed it so. On the contrary, it simply confirms that you—like Nancy, me, and all other human beings—sometimes encounter mysteries of the heart.

Ken Dolan-Del Vecchio & Nancy Saxton-Lopez

Key points

1. Sometimes the grief we feel after the death of a pet feels more intense than any previous grief, even the grief we felt after losing a parent.
2. The daily intimacy that we develop with animal companions and the ways that some of our pets symbolize eras in our lives probably contribute to the intensity of our grief.
3. The fact that we feel this way does not mean that we didn't love or value our human family member enough.

Chapter 6
Why Would Anyone Say Such a Thing?

The unhelpful comments people make vary from misguided attempts at compassion, "He was twelve years old—be thankful that he lived as long as he did," and "He's in a much better place now," to glaringly offensive, "It was only a cat—just get another one!" Some people even suggest that you'll benefit from your pet's death. They say things like, "At least you won't have to spend all your money on vet bills anymore," and, "Look on the bright side, now you're free to travel." Nancy and I will share our thoughts on why people say these things and give suggestions on how you can respond when they do.

What's behind this behavior?

People have complex feelings about animals. Despite the enormous number of companion animals, most people—even many pet owners—continue to see animals as *things*. More specifically, they see animals as things used for food and clothing (leather, fur). At times, animals become ornamental things or entertaining things, as in zoos, rodeos, and SeaWorld. This mentality turns your living, breathing friend into an object that's interchangeable with other similar objects. Hence, "Just get another one!"

Another factor is the difficulty many people experience when they get anywhere near painful feelings. They have almost zero tolerance for emotional pain, their own as well as that experienced by others. Much in our culture promotes this discomfort.

Where in our television shows, movies, songs, and other media do you find people sharing their sad, frightened, vulnerable, or despairing feelings with compassionate listeners? Happy people are *in*. Sad people are *out*. Winners are happy. Sadness is for losers. And, anyway, aren't there pills to take care of that sort of "problem?" Of course I exaggerate, but not very much I'm afraid.

Living with these kinds of messages day in and day out, it makes sense that many people avoid sadness. And when you're taught to avoid sadness, you don't know what to do with it, and, ultimately, sadness ends up scaring you. People don't want you to feel sad because being near you places them at risk of feeling a bit sad themselves. Consequently, "Try to look on the bright side, now you'll have more time for travel and you won't have to pay vet bills and you won't have to clean up after an animal and you won't have to clean fur off your clothing, etc."

Of course, the fact that you feel the way you do, that you're grieving so strongly for your pet, marks you as a person who has resisted this insanity. I'd like to stress, however, that the people who make these kinds of comments do not generally make them out of any negative intentions. Most of what they say comes from sincere wishes for your happiness. In other words, behind layers of confusion and misconception, these comments originate in kindness.

Nancy and I believe that most people want to help. Sometimes, however, they simply have no good ideas on where to begin. The suggestions that follow will help you invite them to get on a better track.

How you can respond

Honesty, directness, and a calm delivery style work best. The last one, calm delivery, lays the cornerstone for success. When you have to communicate something that will be difficult to hear, the way you say it makes all the difference in the world. We have long held the belief that you can deliver even the most challenging messages and likely get a positive result if you pay careful attention to *how you say it*.

Let's say that your coworker notices you've been crying and asks if she can help. You thank her and then explain that your cat died a week ago and every now and then, even when you're at work, you can't help getting a little teary.

She says, "Wow, it was only a cat, right? Why not just go to the shelter and get a new cat?"

You're thinking, "Wow, I had no idea she was such a cold-hearted buffoon," but you bite your tongue. You say, "I'm surprised at your comment. It felt good when you asked if you could help, but when you went on to say, 'It was only a cat, why not just get another one,' that really hurt. I'm sure you didn't mean to hurt me, but just imagine what it would feel like if you were crying over the death of a friend and I said, 'Can't you get another friend?' It would feel a lot better to hear something like, 'I'm sorry that you're going through a rough time.'"

Suppose your brother who lives in a distant city calls you up to see how you're doing, and you tell him that your dog died.

In response he says, "It must be a relief to be out from under those vet bills and having to make sure he get those pills every day. Hey, maybe you can come visit us now that you're not tied down anymore!"

You're thinking, "If he were in front of me right now I would be clasping my hands firmly around his throat," but you take a deep breath and say, "I guess you're trying to help but I'm kind of shocked by your comment. You're right that I devoted a lot of money and time to his care, but that's what you do for a family member who's ill, right? Can we back up and maybe you can say something like, 'It must be hard right now, I know how much Stanley meant to you?'"

It can help to spoon-feed words to people who you believe really do care about you and want to help. You work from the assumption that they didn't say something helpful because they didn't know how. It becomes an act of kindness to give them words that will serve their intended purpose.

Ken Dolan-Del Vecchio & Nancy Saxton-Lopez

These responses can help people grasp how their comments missed the mark. However, you may not feel strong enough at present for such direct confrontation. You may feel that the person you're talking with will get defensive and you don't want to take that on in your current frame of mind. If such is the case, you can always say, "I'll think about what you said and plan to talk with you about it another time."

Your feelings deserve respect

You offer people corrections because your feelings, as well as the feelings of other people, matter. Everybody's feelings deserve respectful handling. When you respond in the ways described above, you give yourself the gift of self-respect and you give the person who made the unfortunate remark a second chance.

If they follow your lead, you may have taught them something valuable. If they don't—if they trivialize your response or tell you that you're being too sensitive or respond in any other manner that shows continued disrespect— then they have taught you something valuable. You have learned that you cannot trust them with your grief. From that moment forward, you will be wise to avoid showing them your feelings and sharing with them any thoughts about your loss. The last thing you need during this challenging time is more hurt.

We live in a world that teaches many people to think of animals as objects, and emotional pain as something to be avoided. This unfortunate state of affairs contributes to a great deal of insensitivity. You may receive, as a result, comments that range from mildly insensitive to outrageously offensive. It can be an act of kindness to give people who say hurtful things the benefit of the doubt, let them know what it felt like to be on the receiving end, and offer them words that would feel supportive instead of upsetting. If they catch on, then you've helped them. If they continue to behave disrespectfully, then you deserve to shield yourself from further exposure to their insensitivity.

Key points

1. People sometimes respond to grieving pet guardians with unexpected insensitivity.
2. This may result from longstanding traditions that give animals the status of objects (rather than living beings) and teach us to fear emotional pain.
3. Your feelings and those of other people deserve respectful handling.
4. It may help to offer a correction that's communicated honestly, directly, and calmly.
5. If insensitivity continues, it makes sense to stop sharing your grief with the offending person.

Chapter 7
All Living Things Die

Blind for two years and deaf longer than that, the curly miniature schnauzer-poodle mix had rarely found the energy to rise and walk during the past five days. She'd eaten almost nothing in as long. The cancer diagnosed three years ago had recently invaded Haddy's mouth and throat, inflaming her snout to twice its normal size and limiting both her airway and her ability to swallow. Three weeks ago, her veterinarian argued that Haddy lived so wracked by pain from her late stage cancer that it was time to let her go. His plea had fallen upon deaf ears as Haddy's people, Jasmine and Gil, had preferred to believe that she would rally back to health. Haddy slipped away in the back seat without making a sound.

Jasmine and Gil were traveling east on Interstate 376 thirteen miles outside of Pittsburgh on their way home to New Jersey from a weekend visit with Jasmine's parents. Twenty minutes later, Jasmine glanced into the back seat as she drove.

"Haddy!" she wailed in a tone that Gil would later describe as "unlike any sound I'd heard her make during our ten years of marriage."

Jasmine stomped on the brake, careened their Subaru into the breakdown lane, slammed the car to a halt, and dove into the back seat.

"I grabbed her snout, closed my mouth over her nose the best I could and started blowing: puff one, puff two, rest one, puff one, puff two, rest one. Blood and spit was spraying from her nose and out the sides of her mouth. I was screaming, NO, NO, NO, NO! I think Gil was afraid I would have a heart attack. He was holding my shoulders and trying to calm me down. We shouldn't have been so far away from home and from her vet. We shouldn't have let her die."

The three group members who had attended any one of the last three of our twice-monthly pet loss groups had heard this story before. Tears streamed down Jasmine's face as she dabbed them with a crumpled tissue. Gil sat next to her, his hands clasped tightly together, his forearms resting on his knees. With his eyes narrowed but not entirely shut and jaws clenched in a grimace, Gil seemed locked in position.

I fixed Jasmine's eyes with mine and spoke in a tone I hoped kind yet resolute. "Your dear friend was in terrible pain. She could not see, could not hear, could barely move, and the cancer in her skull prevented her from breathing. It's important to face the fact that Haddy's death was a necessity, not something you could or should have delayed. Haddy had reached a time that will come to every one of us—she needed to die."

I have conversations like this regularly, although often with a less dramatic start. Such talks have become necessary because we live in a society that denies the inevitability of death. This leads, predictably, to a great deal of confusion on the subject. Medical technology that can prolong life far beyond what would have been imaginable even a generation ago adds to our confusion. Such technological wizardry, while enormously beneficial to countless people and companion animals, has created the illusion that death can be put off indefinitely.

We can buy into the illusion because most of us see little of death in our daily lives. We live so far removed from the natural world, where the facts of life remain undeniably evident, that death has become an unfamiliar trespasser in our lives. Thus, many of us lose touch with the fact that *death is a normal part of life*. Like Jasmine and Gil, we may see even the most predictable end of a long life as a battle or an unexpected horror.

In the vast majority of circumstances, the death of our pet does not mean that we have failed to care for him or her properly or that a veterinarian has failed in his or her responsibility toward their patient or that something else has gone terribly wrong. No, death does not have to mean failure or catastrophe. Instead, death most often means that our friend's life simply has come to an end as all lives eventually do. Each one of us: you, your pets, Nancy, me, and all other living beings on this planet will die one day just as surely as we breathe this very moment.

I emphasize this fact not to upset you but, rather, with exactly the opposite intention. I raise this point because the more we recognize death as a normal, inevitable feature of life, the better prepared we become to make end-of-life decisions, help ourselves heal following the death of a loved one, and help others heal as well.

In the story that opened this chapter, Jasmine and Gil's inability to face the reality of Haddy's rapidly approaching death, though undoubtedly driven by the most loving motivation, created unnecessary pain for everybody involved. When we accept death as a normal event, we no longer need to battle against it. Had Jasmine and Gil either made the decision to euthanize Haddy or, as an alternative, keep her comfortably medicated through her last days, they could have said goodbye to their pet over time in a calm and loving manner. She may have died at her home or vet's office surrounded by loving people, rather than alone in the back seat of their car. The couple would have spared themselves the jarring drama described by Jasmine so many times at pet loss meetings.

None of us welcomes the death of a loved one, but denying that it will happen doesn't help. Even when we do not face a challenge like the one that confronted Jasmine and Gil, recognizing the reality of death offers benefits. These include the likelihood that we will value life even more highly. We may embrace the life expectancy of members of our pet's species as a reminder of the preciousness of time spent together. Similarly, we may embrace the life expectancy of our own species as a reminder to live our own lives with great attention to purpose. Finally, when we accept that every

Ken Dolan-Del Vecchio & Nancy Saxton-Lopez

life comes to an end, we become better equipped to help others, including our children, manage their grief.

Key points

1. Death is the normal, inevitable conclusion to life, not necessarily a failure, accident, or catastrophe.
2. Seeing death in this manner frees us to provide comfort, support, and fond goodbyes instead of mounting an ultimately futile battle against forces beyond our control.
3. Accepting death can help us value our lives and the lives of those whom we love.
4. Recognizing death as a part of life can help us help others, including our children.

Chapter 8

Many People Agonize Over the Decision to Euthanize

I'd like to share with you how my spouse and I decided to euthanize our cat, Reginald. I've told the story several times at pet loss groups, and repeat it now because it feels important to tell a personal story and not someone else's. After all, euthanasia doesn't happen at third-person distance. It happens at close range, closer to hand and heart than the two Chihuahuas sprawled next to my keyboard as I type these words. This very personal decision—loaded with uncertainty and guilt, and yet a godsend when your pet faces terminal suffering—may be one of the most difficult ones you'll make. Here's how it went for us.

For five months we'd known about the cancer invading every part of Reggie's body. Still, we'd tried our best to push aside thoughts of the inevitable. You see, Reggie's stoicism made our denial easy.

He still followed us everywhere around the house, meowing his approval at each opening of the refrigerator door and relishing the tidbits to follow. He still rushed ahead of us into every room as though providing security clearance. He still made sure to settle beside one or the other of us, whether we were writing bills at our desk, settling into the couch to read, or chatting on the telephone. He ate with the same gusto as the fuzzy ball of tan and white who had arrived home with us from the "I Love Animals" shelter ten short years earlier.

He still slept between us stretched out like a little nine-pound person, his head resting right between ours in the valley where our pillows met. Here he'd purr and doze until I'd fallen into that state just before real sleep takes hold. Then without fail Reggie would ever-so-gently box the tip of my nose, the pads of his feet brushing with just enough force to pull me back awake. I'd mumble "No, Reggie!" and shift position. He'd brush my nose again. My spouse would giggle.

All this had changed abruptly in the last week, however. We couldn't avoid commenting on his sudden drop in weight, sluggishness, loss of appetite, and the foul smell that now seemed a part of him. The vet told us the smell was "normal" with cancer. It rose from dying flesh.

We struggled to decide when to help him die, that time when discomfort *irreversibly* outweighs the pleasures of living. Fate delivered a signal. We awoke one morning to find that a lesion had burst onto the left side of Reggie's mouth. Dumbfounded, we stared at Reggie as he drooled and pawed at the grey-black tissue. He shook his head and then pushed his mouth to the floor, still pawing at his face. Hindquarters raised and head pinned to the floor, he spun his body around, trying to rid himself of the thing. Reggie's eyes flashed, opened impossibly wide, and silently wailed his panic.

Saying little to each other, my spouse and I took turns dressing ourselves and comforting Reggie. We called the babysitter to look after our one-year-old son and prepared for the drive to our vet's office.

Dr. Howard Almer, Reggie's veterinarian, examined him and confirmed the obvious. The new lesion marked the cancer's progression. Howard told us that it was difficult to assess whether Reggie's pawing at the lesion was caused more by pain or by his distress at feeling the growth's presence on his lip and face. He suggested that the way Reggie pawed at it—something that he continued to do while on the examining table—suggested some degree of pain.

Howard advised us that he could prescribe pain-killers and sedatives to lessen Reggie's distress, suggesting that these might buy several days of relative calm. He also encouraged us to look at the overall picture. "Reggie has eaten almost nothing during the past several days, his energy level has fallen sharply, and now he's got this lesion on his face and lip causing him worry and possibly pain. I don't expect this new development will bode well for his desire to eat. It's your decision to make, but we know your friend has nowhere to go but downhill from here and this morning he may have passed the tipping point where pain and discomfort outweigh the benefits of living."

We decided that medicating Reggie to calm him down so he could stay with us a few more days would serve *our* interests more than *his*. We asked Howard to end his suffering.

We held and stroked Reggie, who lay on the blanket we'd brought with us, while Howard gave the injection. Reggie slipped away with little movement, without a sound. We stayed with his body for a half hour, crying, holding one another, then talking over the past several days.

During the time that followed, we agonized over Reggie's final days. Had we waited too long and prolonged his suffering unnecessarily? Did we put enough thought into the decision to end his life? Should we have taken him home and thought it over more carefully? Should we have sought another opinion? Why didn't we notice that growth while it was just a small lesion inside his lip— could it have been removed surgically if we'd paid more attention and caught it sooner? Would this have given him another month? Should we really have stayed with him when the vet put him to sleep? Did Reggie think that we killed him? Should we instead have said our goodbyes and left the room until he was gone?

Through time and conversation with one another, family members, and friends, we came to understand that euthanizing a pet almost always leaves guardians reeling with questions of this sort. (Incidentally, guardians whose pets die *without* the assistance of euthanasia often find themselves posing very similar questions.) We learned to see our need to ask these questions over and over again as part of the normal uncertainty that comes with grief. And we struggled to accept that our best judgment remains imperfect: our decision to euthanize based upon our love for our friend, the knowledge we had at the time, and the wisest counsel available.

At age twelve, Nancy's pug, Noelle, who had been slowly losing the use of her back legs as the result of a congenital spinal defect, suddenly lost functioning in all four legs. Many people advised Nancy and her husband to euthanize Noelle, despite the fact that she remained alert, happy, and apparently pain-free. Assured by Noelle's veterinarian that she felt no pain, Nancy and her husband decided that, rather than euthanize her, they would become Noelle's legs. They carried her about: in and out of the house so she could do her business and from room to room so she could stay near one or the other of them, and they fed her by hand. Noelle loved the attention, making it known when she wanted a tummy rub or a roll on the carpet.

This arrangement worked for more than a year, whereupon Noelle developed a tumor in her chest that made breathing difficult. Noelle's veterinarian advised that she likely felt no discomfort as a result of the tumor but its inevitable growth would ultimately prevent her from breathing. He advised that Noelle be euthanized at the point at which her difficulty breathing overwhelmed her ability to experience the pleasures of eating and being with her family.

As had been grimly predicted, Noelle's breathing became increasingly labored. After much discussion one evening, Nancy and her husband scheduled Noelle's final veterinary appointment for the following morning. They spent that night lovingly talking with Noelle about times they'd shared. Both accompanied Noelle in the morning, holding her as she passed from consciousness.

Being present when euthanasia is administered

While many people choose to stay with their pet during euthanasia, many others choose to wait in another room. Like so much about loss and grieving, the right decision is the one that feels best to you and your loved ones. When children say they want to be present, a responsible adult needs to lend their judgment and make the final decision. Seeing their pet's final moments pass quietly and without evidence of pain or distress can be helpful to people of all ages. Some people, children among them, experience such great anxiety, however, that being present would heighten rather than lessen their pain. For them, waiting in another room makes more sense.

Whether your pet's last breath takes place in the same room as the one in which you stand undoubtedly matters far less than the lifetime of love and care you've provided. The truth of that statement will not prevent some people from rehashing their decision countless times, however. Such is the nature of grief.

Nancy often reminds people that deciding to euthanize means deciding to end suffering rather than deciding to kill. Your pet experiences their final moments here not as a time of betrayal but as moments in which your care for them continues. Trust is not betrayed but, rather, fulfilled by your decision to provide an easier transition. Euthanasia brings a small degree of control over when and how death will occur. Responsibility for death itself belongs to illness, infirmity, and mortality, forces well beyond your control.

Key points:
1. When making end-of-life decisions, involve people you trust, including your pet's veterinarian.
2. The most helpful question: *Does irreversible suffering outweigh the benefits of living?*
3. If possible, have another person who you love and respect with you at the time of your pet's euthanasia.
4. Expect second-guessing no matter how carefully you made the decision.

Chapter 9

Helping Children after the Loss of a Pet

Every parent wants to protect their child from pain, including the pain of grief. Nevertheless, death and other losses inevitably happen. We can't completely shield our children and when we try to do so we miss opportunities to help them build resilience. We also invite unintended consequences that can make matters worse.

Facts like these don't stand in the way of some people, however. Two years ago I consulted with an executive and his wife who had learned that morning of the death of his mother, a woman in her seventies who had seemed a picture of health. This man and his wife had two children, aged six and seven. While the children's grandmother had lived in Massachusetts, a distance from their home in New Jersey, the kids enjoyed rich relationships with her. They spoke to Grandma on the telephone at least once a week and she visited regularly.

Before I spoke with them, the couple had decided that they would hide Grandma's death from their children. They had concocted a tale that saw Grandma setting off on a year-long, around-the-world cruise. The couple told me they would inform the kids that Grandma scheduled her departure with such haste that she had time only for a quick call to her son asking that he give her love to all. After a year they imagined Grandma might decide to continue her adventure in some far-off land, perhaps signing on for a stint with the Peace Corps. The couple had convinced themselves that eventually their children would forget their grandmother.

While at first I took what they told me as evidence of the numbing confusion that can follow news of a loved one's unexpected death, two days later the plan remained unchanged. In fact, now the story had been embellished in order to conceal the funeral in Massachusetts. Dad would be flying away on an "urgent business trip" and Mom had decided to accompany him, while a babysitter would stay with the kids for the next several days.

While I had tried gentle persuasion during our first consultation, this time I adopted a more challenging tone. I asked the couple why they preferred to tell their kids that Grandma had abandoned them rather than help them adjust to the fact of her death. I assured them that they would not spare the children grief with this lie. On the contrary, their story would double their children's grief: They would grieve over Grandma's disappearance and they would also grieve over her apparent lack of regard for them.

I advised that the children would likely wonder what they'd done to cause their grandmother to reject them, as children readily assume they bear responsibility for the circumstances in which they find themselves. I also wondered aloud about how the children would react when they eventually discovered the truth.

Finally, I told the couple that, while I knew it would make them terribly sad to share the truth with the children and they surely didn't need additional challenges at present, I would help them manage. I assured them that this would be the best course of action for all involved. Tears gathered in their eyes and they remained silent for a few moments. Then both parents agreed and we began planning how to break the news to their children.

It's never easy to see our children in pain. When we become parents, however, we sign on for a host of new responsibilities, including the duty to help our children live through the loss of loved ones, some of whom will be pets. The sections that follow offer guidance that can help.

Inform and include them

First of all, don't make the mistake almost made by the couple described above. Include your children. Share news of a pet's death in a way that fits their stage of development. Although children, like adults, vary tremendously, it can help to keep the following in mind. Very young children, those younger than five years old, cannot grasp the meaning of death in the same way as adults. They have difficulty understanding permanence. When you explain what has happened to your pet, it can help to talk about their death in simple and specific terms.

"Bosley died. He stopped moving and eating and hearing and seeing. He won't wake up again. His body won't work anymore. We're all going to miss him."

An explanation of this sort helps very young children because without it they may fear, as one possibility, that after a pet's body has been buried the pet may awaken and find themselves buried alive. Even after hearing this explanation and seeing their pet's dead body, children of this age may ask repeatedly when their pet will be coming back. You may need to patiently repeat the explanation above, gently emphasizing that their friend will not be returning in the future.

By age eight or nine, most children have begun to grasp the meaning of death in a more adult fashion. They know that death means the irreversible end of life.

Whatever you and your family choose to do with your pet's body, and we'll discuss a variety of options in Chapter Ten, it's a good idea to keep your child informed. If you create a ritual, such as a funeral, it makes sense to invite your child to participate.

Assure children that they are not responsible for the pet's death

As mentioned earlier, children of all ages, even early adolescents, often assume that they bear at least some degree of responsibility for unhappy family events, and the younger the child, the greater the likelihood of this happening. That's why Nancy and I recommend setting them straight: "This may sound a little strange because you probably already know, but I'm going to say it anyway to be certain. When unhappy things happen in their families, kids tend to feel like they may be the cause. I want you to know that nothing you did had anything to do with Jake's death. Many times kids think things like 'if I worked harder at school or behaved better at home or spent more time with him this wouldn't have happened.' If you're thinking anything like that, you're wrong. Jake was a very old dog and he had lots of health problems—that's why he died."

Children learn by watching their parents and other adults

Children learn how to deal with the death of their pet mostly by watching their parents and the other adults in their lives. Let me stress that *children watch what we do*. And if what we do contradicts what we say, they pay more attention to our actions. You know how this works if you've ever worked for a boss who says "make sure you take your lunch break" and "feel free to leave at five o'clock" but then never takes a lunch break and routinely stays much later than five o'clock herself. It doesn't matter what she says because her actions tell a different story. On the other hand, if you work for a boss who leaves his desk for an hour every noontime and leaves work every day at five o'clock so he can be with his family, he doesn't have to say a word. You know that you can do the same. Keep this in mind and act accordingly. You will become an extraordinarily helpful role model for your child.

The death of a family pet launches a difficult but important life lesson for your child. If your pet had been sick for some time, the lesson began even earlier as your child watched and, perhaps, participated in the care-giving and concern. If you faced a decision about euthanasia, you may have kept him or her informed as the decision-making progressed. Your child may or may not have been present at the time of death. If you or your child discovered your pet's lifeless body, your child undoubtedly remembers how you reacted to that discovery and how you helped them through the moment.

Your child watches everything you do, including how you handle information about the loss. Do you share news of your pet's death freely and openly or has their death become something that you never mention, unspeakable in other words? A woman who attended a recent pet loss group described how, following the death of their family dog when she was ten years old, his existence was erased from the family's historical record. Her parents told the kids that they would all be better off if they tried to forget about him. All pictures that included him were discarded, every effort was made to put memories of him aside, and sharing feelings about his death was labeled "rude."

The woman went on to describe how her inability to grieve this loss affected her. She talked about how she tried to apply the "let's forget it ever happened rule" to break-ups with boyfriends and other unwelcome changes. She described the extraordinary relief she felt at present, when the overwhelming pain of losing her last dog compelled her to finally break the rule of silence.

It helps to teach your children that everything, regardless of how upsetting or challenging, can be discussed. When we can talk about something, we diminish its power over us. We make it manageable. Talking allows us to examine what happened and shape our reactions to it together. Ultimately, talking things over helps us locate events, even very painful ones, within the larger story of our lives in a way that makes sense and restores comfort. If we decide that something cannot be discussed, however, we convince children that it is huge, frightening, overwhelming, and completely insurmountable. This undermines their ability to manage loss. It teaches that some things in life, including completely normal events like the death of a pet, can only be managed by denial.

You become the role model for your child when it comes to grieving. He or she watches and takes mental notes on how you share your thoughts, feelings, and questions. Many parents believe that they should demonstrate a calm, completely stoic disposition. Their thinking goes something like this: *while I feel like crying on the inside, I have to appear strong and in control so my child doesn't feel like I'm falling apart and they've got nobody who they can depend on.*

Nancy and I agree that parents should not dissolve into wild, wailing, bouts of grief that last for several minutes when they are alone with their child. Such behavior will likely panic the child and serve no good purpose. However, when a parent shows no distressed feelings at all and, instead, only the most composed demeanor throughout the days that follow the death of the family's pet, this can make an unfortunate impact as well. A child who has been terribly saddened by the loss will feel more distressed and alone than if the parent showed similar feelings. Remember, when you say, "This makes me really sad, too," that means far less to a child than when *your actions demonstrate sadness.*

Experience taught me that an honest sharing of my own grief for a lost pet worked well when helping my son, Erik, through his grief. When Erik was eight years old his Mini Rex rabbit, Doris, took ill one afternoon. Doris had free run of Erik's room. When we were all at home she had free run of the house. She was house-trained. She reliably returned to her cage to eat, drink, poop and pee. Doris was Erik's pal. He'd talk to her before falling asleep at night and she received his first greeting every morning. Doris had never before shown any sign of ill health. That afternoon, she passed diarrhea repeatedly and sat nearly motionless, grinding her teeth, a sign of pain in rabbits. We took her to the veterinarian for an emergency visit. He prescribed some medication and sent us home.

The next morning Doris seemed much better. By early evening, however, her condition was deteriorating. We were ready to leave for the vet's office when she stretched out, shuddered several times, and died. Erik petted her quietly and tears came to his eyes. I petted her as well and tears came to my eyes. I hugged Erik and told him how sorry I was that Doris died. He hugged me back very tightly and sobbed as he buried his face in my shoulder. We both sobbed while petting Doris some more. She was stretched out in a position not much different from the one she sometimes assumed while sleeping. I gently closed her eyelids.

Erik and I called his mom to tell her the sad news and begin to plan for Doris' burial. I told Erik that I thought we might put Doris's body in a box and not leave her where she was on her bed. He liked that idea. I set her body in a shoebox and he placed some of her chew sticks and hay beside her. He told me that he wanted to put some hay in the box because Doris loved eating hay so much. We both cried and hugged on and off as we settled her body in the box. By sharing my own tears, I invited Erik to do the same. If I had remained stoic he would have felt all alone in his sadness. Children mirror the behavior of their parents and other adults. Showing them our grief, we provide reassurance and support.

Help children express themselves

Some children, my son among them, express their thoughts and feelings freely. They love to talk about what's on their minds, good or bad. Other children grow very quiet when they're hurting. Many children of all ages respond well to suggestions that they create a card or other artwork to honor and say goodbye to their pet. As with adults, it won't help to pressure your child into sharing their feelings. Instead, create opportunities and let them decide.

Erik has had cats in his family since he was born. We gave him a kitten, who he named Willy, when he was seven years old. Willy died tragically not even two years later. She had gotten into a crawl space that, unbeknownst to us, had been seeded with rat poison by the property's previous owner.

The tradition in our family for saying goodbye to a deceased pet usually centers on a brief "funeral service" that we hold just before burying the body. At Willy's funeral, each of us read goodbye cards. Erik read his card: "Thank you for being such a good friend, Willy. I wish we had a longer time to be friends and I'll always remember you."

He had decorated the card with drawings of "Erik carrying Willy," "Willy chasing a string that Erik pulls," and "Willy and me playing hide and seek." Erik, his mom, and I cried as we read our cards and listened to one another.

Provide choices

Providing a child with choices can help. For example, if your five-year-old announces that she's too sad to go to bed, you can give her the choice of staying up for another half hour or going to bed now and hearing you read two stories instead of the usual one. You may give your ten-year-old son the choice of whether or not to come to the vet's office when the family dog will be euthanized. You may also give him the option of remaining in the waiting room with his other parent or being present during his dog's last moments. Your seven-year-old can be told that he can decide whether the family should store his dog's bed in the basement or leave it where it's always been at the foot of his bed for the time being. Providing these kinds of choices conveys respect for your child's feelings while also helping to restore his or her sense of personal control at a time when it feels like much control has been lost.

Regression is normal

Sometimes after the death of a pet, or indeed after any other extraordinarily stressful change, children revert to behaviors from earlier developmental stages. For example, a six-year-old girl who no longer sucks her thumb may pick up the habit again for a brief period of time following the death of her pet. An eight-year-old boy who hasn't wet the bed in years may do so again after losing the dog he'd known all of his life and considered his very best friend.

These temporary regressions can be a normal part of grief. Take them as signs of the child's distress and offer as much support as you can. In the case of a child sucking his or her thumb or talking in a baby-talk style long after you thought this stage had passed, it may be best not to describe what they're doing but rather just note that you can see how sad they feel.

"Julie, you look like you're feeling pretty upset. Can I give you a big hug?"

It's wise to avoid mentioning the thumb-sucking or baby talk because doing so will most likely embarrass the child. Their embarrassment will only increase how upset they feel, causing them to demonstrate *even more* of the thumb-sucking or baby talk in order to soothe themselves further. Simply offering lots of support goes right to the heart of the matter without causing additional distress.

When regression takes the form of bedwetting or nightmares, it can help to reassure the child not to worry.

"Don't worry, Tommy, stuff like this happens when kids are going through a tough time, like all of us are after losing Bowser. Let's get your sheets changed so you can go back to sleep."

We've described elsewhere how adults sometimes find themselves needing to hold one of their deceased pet's toys in order to fall asleep, or they purchase life-sized stuffed animals and place them in their own beds where their pets used to sleep. These examples show that people of all ages sometimes regress when they're grieving, not just children. All of us sometimes soothe ourselves by behaving in ways typical of an earlier, less complicated time in our lives.

Few responsibilities prove more challenging than parenting. We must help our children learn all the skills needed for a fulfilling life. Coping with death ranks high among them. We rightly strive to prevent our children from facing unnecessary suffering—the suffering that, for example, comes from illness, neglect, violence, bullying, discrimination, and poor nutrition. Death and other losses, however, cannot be prevented. Therefore, grief, the passage from loss to healing, can be thought of as *necessary* suffering. We can't prevent our children from facing this kind of suffering but we can help them learn to care for themselves through its duration. In doing so, we teach skills that will serve them throughout their lives.

Ken Dolan-Del Vecchio & Nancy Saxton-Lopez

Key points

1. Your children will pay close attention to how you deal with the loss personally. Your actions provide the model for how they'll approach their own grief.

2. Share your sadness honestly. Cry if you feel like crying. Your honest display, as long as it doesn't rise to the level of panic, will help your child feel less alone with his or her own sadness.

3. Include children. Tell them the facts of the loss and include them in plans for saying goodbye. Keep in mind that if you don't inform your children they will fantasize to fill the gaps in information. Their fantasies may be more painful than the truth.

4. Providing your child with choices will help them feel more in control at a time when this can be very helpful.

5. Handle any regression in behavior with thoughtful regard for how to help your child feel supported and not embarrassed.

Chapter 10

Deciding What to Do with Your Pet's Body

When a human family member dies we often have a ready-made plan, sometimes even including specific instructions left by the deceased. The plan may follow long-held religious, cultural, and family traditions. Not so when a pet dies. While some pet guardians plan in advance, many others must decide what to do with their friend's body without the benefit of forethought. This chapter examines the question in some detail, presenting a range of views and some options for your consideration.

To start, let's identify the concerns that guide how people have traditionally managed human remains. These can help us evaluate the choices for a pet's body.

We dispose of our fellow human beings' bodies in ways that serve three major purposes. The first is sanitation. We use methods designed to prevent health hazards, primarily burying deep within the earth and cremation, which renders the body as sanitary ashes. Second, we treat human remains in ways that we consider respectful. We handle them with special care. Finally, we may feature the remains in a memorial ritual, or funeral, that helps us acknowledge the loss, celebrate the person's life, and move ahead with our grief. Depending upon our spirituality, the funeral may also serve to entrust the deceased person's soul to the care of divinity. Summing up, the main considerations that help us decide what to do with a human being's body after death are sanitation, respectful handling, and ceremonial importance. Let's discuss how these apply to a deceased pet.

Ken Dolan-Del Vecchio & Nancy Saxton-Lopez

Sanitary concerns

Few of us would argue the importance of sanitation. If a pet's body requires storage for any length of time, refrigeration or freezing must be employed. Nancy and I have encountered people who for a matter of days kept their pet's dead body in their garage, bedroom, and in one case (with a fish) under their pillow. The results in each case were unpleasant to say the least. Many veterinarians will agree to hold your pet's body in their freezer if you need time to decide your next step. If your pet was extremely large, such as a horse, donkey, or large breed of dog, you will likely need special assistance. Your veterinarian, a pet crematory business, or your local animal shelter can provide guidance.

Many points of view

The definition of respectful handling and the degree of ceremonial importance people assign their pet's body varies. When it comes to these two considerations, pet guardians usually can't rely upon family or cultural traditions as they can when a human family member dies. Our traditions, for the most part, have had little to say about pets. Instead, we have to decide what feels most comfortable for us.

At one end of the spectrum people feel that after their pet has died it doesn't matter what happens to the body. They see their friend's physical remains somewhat like the empty chrysalis discarded by a butterfly after emerging, stretching her wings, and flying off. All that was alive and beautiful has gone and only an empty shell remains. These people may simply want their pet's remains disposed of in a sanitary fashion. They may leave the details to their veterinarian. Or they may take it upon themselves to bury their pet's body in their own back yard, local ordinances permitting. Some may wrap the body in plastic and dispose of it with their household trash. They mean no disrespect. They simply no longer identify their pet, the spirit who was their dear friend, with the body that remains behind after death.

At the other end of the spectrum people ensure that their pet's body gets handled with the same reverence that they'd require for a human family member. They honor their pet's remains as the most precious representation of their departed friend, sometimes devoting a great deal of time and money to ensure the delivery of extraordinary care.

People who feel this way may arrange for a funeral service, available today through many pet memorial businesses, which includes all the ceremonial features associated with funerals provided for human beings. They may decide upon a burial plot within a pet cemetery and mark the site with a granite or marble headstone.

As an alternative to cremation or burial, some people have their pet's body preserved through taxidermy or freeze drying. The latter, a relatively new and costly technology, dehydrates the body. It preserves the size and appearance of the animal as he or she looked when alive. The body thus transformed can be kept on display indefinitely.

Other pet owners fall somewhere in the middle on this continuum. For example, some people purchase group cremation, which means that their pet's body is incinerated along with other bodies. These pet guardians want cremation and they like the idea of their pet's ashes being scattered on a pet cemetery's memorial lawn. They feel no desire, however, to retrieve the ashes and no discomfort having their pet's ashes mixed with those of other animals.

Deciding what feels right

What course of action feels most comforting and practical for you? Let this become your guiding question. Allow your emotional needs, your budget, and the loving counsel of family and friends who understand how much this means to you help you decide. Remember that there are no correct and incorrect answers here, only options that suit your feelings more or less well.

Incidentally, people do not always choose to dispose of all of their pets' bodies in the same ways. The choice made often depends upon the circumstances of the moment. As an adult I had buried in my back yard the bodies of each of our cats and dogs. When our dog, Lily, died, however, it felt more fitting to have her cremated. Her ashes now rest in a ceramic box on top of my dresser.

Practicality can become the primary consideration. Nancy and I have heard many people say that they cannot bury their pet on their property because they would feel badly were they to change residences. They therefore decide to bury their pets at pet memorial parks or cremate and keep the ashes inside their homes. Apartment dwellers may not have access to land and so cannot bury their pets. Many people ask their veterinarian to dispose of the body because this is the most economical way to manage expenses or because it happens to be winter, the ground is frozen, and they can't imagine how they would dig a grave.

One couple debated for weeks over whether they would cremate or freeze dry their Dachshund. Nancy suggested that perhaps they should freeze dry and see how they felt about the result as they could always decide to cremate thereafter. (Of course, the reverse order would not be an option.) This suggestion helped them move forward with the decision and with their grieving.

Nancy's example shows how important it becomes, when a pet leaves behind more than one guardian, for the survivors to negotiate lovingly with one another. When disagreements arise, we suggest that together you decide who feels most strongly about the method of disposal. It then becomes a kind gesture for those who feel less strongly to yield to the person to whom this matters most.

It may help to allow yourself a specific time frame for making your decision. One woman found the thought of saying a final goodbye to her deceased dog unbearably painful. Finally, nearly eighteen months after his death, she scheduled a funeral service and burial at a pet memorial park. The staff thawed and groomed her pet's body, placed it in a casket, and delivered a service that she found deeply gratifying but also unexpectedly disturbing, as she had not seen her pet's body for such a long time. While we can't be certain, Nancy and I wondered whether she might have eased the duration of her grieving had she scheduled her dog's funeral earlier.

Involve only carefully chosen people

Because many people discount the lives of animals, you may face unpleasantness from some people if you mention your pet's cremation, memorial service, or burial. As we've recommended elsewhere in this book, you can avoid additional distress by discussing these matters only with carefully chosen support people. Remember that the purpose of your decision is to aide healing and not to win arguments or convert people who think differently.

Closely related to your decision regarding the disposal of your pet's body is the question of whether or not to mark their passing with a formal ritual—a funeral. The following chapter addresses this question.

Key points

1. Sanitation is an essential concern. If you need time to decide what to do with your pet's body, place it in a freezer. Your veterinarian or a pet memorial business may be able to do this for you.
2. Above all else, allow personal comfort to guide your decision. There are no correct and incorrect methods of disposing of your pet's remains beyond the matter of sanitation.
3. Include all the pet's guardians in the decision-making. If consensus proves difficult to reach, honoring the wishes of the person who seems most concerned with the fate of your pet's body makes for the kindest solution.

Chapter 11

Funerals, Places of Remembrance, and other Memorials

Rituals such as baptisms, graduations, birthday parties, weddings, anniversaries, and funerals help us acknowledge, celebrate, and manage our reactions to change. A ritual's structure—often including music, readings, and other symbolic activities—serves to amplify as well as contain our emotions. At weddings, for example, the music that heralds the beginning of the event, the ceremonial procession, and exchange of vows – all of these elements move us. They stir feelings of joy and hope for the new couple. They also evoke sadness and nostalgia as we reflect upon how quickly time turns infants into young adults, single friends into a married couple, and new love into committed partnership. In the space of an hour or so, the wedding ritual heightens and contains a swell of feelings. Afterward, we return to daily life enriched by the formal acknowledgment of change that we've shared. Because rituals help us make sense of important life transitions, many people decide to have a funeral for their deceased pet.

A funeral for your pet

A funeral can be as simple or as complex as you desire. The ritual typically includes participants reading letters, cards, or short essays that express their feelings for the deceased. Many people include the pet's body (in a box or casket), ashes, or some other representation, often a photo or drawing, as the centerpiece. The funeral may include the reading of prayers or inspirational writings. As I've described earlier, in my family we usually read a goodbye letter and express our thanks for the time we had with our friend. Nancy often recommends the funeral scene in the movie *Marley and Me* to those seeking a helpful example.

Your pet's funeral may involve symbolic actions that demonstrate love, connection to the universe, and release. Possibilities include lighting candles and letting them burn until they extinguish, releasing a helium-filled balloon, each participant placing a flower on the casket, urn, or pet's photograph, ringing a bell, playing taps or a similarly mournful piece on a musical instrument, lighting incense, drawing in the sand or soil and then smoothing it again, and pouring water, wine, or another beverage onto the ground. Depending upon where you live, you may release small "boats" into a river or ocean.

Design the funeral so that it suits your tastes and honors your relationship with your pet in a way that feels fitting. One man who spent memorable hours with his golden retriever hiking in the Adirondack Mountains placed dried leaves and sticks, reminiscent of the mountain trails they shared, at the base of the photograph that served as the centerpiece for his dog's funeral. Many people feature their pet's favorite toys, collars, and leashes. It can help children to draw a picture to include in the ceremony. As with funerals for human beings, music can make an important contribution.

If you enlist the help of a pet memorial business, they will offer you a variety of options, including in many cases a formal viewing or wake, closed or open casket with your pet's well groomed body on display, and a choice of music and readings.

However you decide to proceed, it can help to keep the ritual fairly brief and follow it with a gathering in a different setting. If the funeral takes place at your pet's gravesite, hold the gathering that follows in your dining room or on the porch or deck, for example. The change of location marks the end of the funeral. In the introduction to this book I mentioned the funeral for Zeke, my childhood best friend's dog. My friend's mother wisely took us kids to an ice cream parlor immediately afterward to shift our focus from the pain of loss to the celebration of memories. "Breaking bread" after your pet's funeral concludes can shift the focus in similar fashion.

A special place for remembrance

Whether you dispose of your pet's body in a way that includes a final resting place or not, you may find it healing to create a special place or object that helps you remember. For some people, their pet's gravesite or the place where ashes were released serves this function. Other people create memorials that do not involve their pet's remains. They may plant a shrub, tree, or memorial garden that commemorates their friend.

The special place can be a memorial display inside your home. As mentioned previously, many people choose to create what they call "altars," often displaying photographs and items that belonged to the pet. A container bearing the pet's ashes or a lock of the pet's hair may be included among these items.

Memorial objects

Some people carry reminders of their lost pet with them at all times. Recently, our pet loss support groups have included people wearing pendants in the form of little canisters that contain a small amount of their pet's ashes. Many people carry photographs of their pets, sometimes inside their purses or wallets and, increasingly, in their cell phones and other electronic devices. Others carry a lock of their pet's hair or the tag that their pet carried on his or her collar identifying their name, address, and guardian's phone number. Some people craft and wear memorial rings or pendants. These items bring great solace to the bearers.

Donations to service organizations

Many people memorialize their pets by making donations in their name to organizations that care for animals in need. These include the American Society for the Prevention of Cruelty to Animals (ASPCA), The Humane Society, local animal shelters, and pet rescue organizations.

It can help to imagine grief as a spiral of healing that moves us to revisit the experience of our loss repeatedly, each time providing us with new perspectives, each time helping us experience our feelings in ways that bring us a step or two toward greater peace. The activities described in this chapter, funeral rituals and the crafting of remembrances, provide points for reflection on that spiral of healing. Some of them will fit your temperament and life circumstances well, and others will not. We offer them as ideas, starting places from which you can build the rituals and remembrances that best suit you and your loved ones.

Key points

1. Many people find it helpful to say a formal goodbye by holding a funeral.
2. It may help to create a special place of remembrance for your pet.
3. Craft rituals and remembrances to fit your temperament and circumstances. As with most other aspects of the grieving process, there are no correct and incorrect methods, only what works best for you.

Chapter 12

Should I Get Another Pet?

Many people who attend pet loss support groups ask if or when it makes sense to bring a new animal companion into their life. As you may imagine, our answers begin with "it depends." Let's walk through some of the points to consider.

Assess your motivation honestly

The pain of grief can be so intense that you may try your hardest to avoid it. Who wants to feel terribly sad if there's a way to leapfrog over the pain? Sometimes people imagine that getting another pet will make this happen. They may not be so naïve as to think the new pet will replace the one they've lost and make their grief disappear, but they imagine that caring for their new friend will distract them enough to end their grief. If you fit this description, please think again.

If you act from this kind of motivation, instead of filling the void left by your deceased friend, the presence of the newcomer may do exactly the opposite. The new addition, who cannot help the fact that he or she differs from their predecessor, may amplify your sense of loss. You may also become resentful.

"Suzie never peed on the floor and she was a lot friendlier—what's wrong with you?"

Please don't let this happen.

Instead, honestly evaluate why you want a new pet. It can help to talk things over with someone who can be counted on to level with you. Recognize that when you're grieving, bringing a new companion animal into your home will more likely than not offer both challenges and rewards, and you will still need to grieve for the pet you've lost.

Sometimes the decision to adopt shortly after a loss works out just fine. Many people decide to bring home a new pet because in the absence of their recently departed friend they have the space and resources to care for an animal in need. They welcome this new friend with eyes wide open, expecting that this new pet's presence will at times emphasize their grief and at other times help them feel better.

One woman adopted a shelter kitten two weeks after the death of her cat. Full of energy and a fair amount of trouble (Who knew drapes were for climbing?), the little one brought many smiles to her face. The new kitten also snuggled with her at night, bringing great comfort. She still grieved her loss, but this new friend lessened her sadness.

Timing can make all the difference. Opening your home to a new pet can be a wonderful testament to your deceased friend: He or she gave so much love that you're eager to welcome a new friend as a result. In fairness to both you and your new pet, however, make sure that you're emotionally prepared.

Evaluate your energy level

In addition to the emotional demands, we encourage you also to consider the practical concerns. If your deceased pet was an adult dog, for example, and you have just been offered the opportunity to adopt an eight-week-old puppy, please remember how much work goes into training. Puppies require a lot more from us than well-trained, mature dogs. Grief tends to lessen our energy reserves and it will not help to invite more stress into your life at present.

Avoid impulse decisions

Now more than ever, you need to protect yourself from impulse decisions. The emotional roller coaster of grief can make us prone to flash decision-making. Beware. Steer clear of pet stores and animal shelters until more time has passed if you feel vulnerable in this regard.

As with all matters that affect other members of your household, be sure to include them in this decision. If your spouse or children want more time, heed their feelings. You can always postpone getting a new pet, but you wouldn't want to return one who you've brought into your home. Getting a new pet will always be a momentous decision. Making the decision thoughtfully will benefit everyone involved.

Let time be your friend

As you grieve, please embrace time as a friend. Time proves essential to healing the pain of grief, and when it comes to deciding about a new pet, similarly, time stands firmly on your side. A delay will cause no harm. Instead, it will help you clarify any confusion.

The appropriate amount of time between the death of one pet and the adoption of another varies according to the factors discussed above. As with so many other matters related to grieving, there exists no simple formula. What's right for you may not work for another person.

Temperaments and life situations factor into determining what's best for any given individual and family. Many people, including me, always have more than one pet. I currently have three dogs, two rabbits, and three chickens. When one of my pets dies, I may or may not bring another home right away. I make that determination in consultation with my spouse and with consideration for what else happens to be going on within our lives at the time.

Some people swear they'll never get another pet. A few actually mean it. Some make this vow because agonizing grief convinces them that they could not weather such a loss again. Other people, often those of advanced years, decide not to take on the responsibility again because they anticipate moving to a smaller home or their infirmities make it difficult to manage a pet's care. Questions about whether and when to adopt a new pet deserve thoughtful

Ken Dolan-Del Vecchio & Nancy Saxton-Lopez

consideration of your needs and life circumstances, and it always helps to discuss the pros and cons with loved ones.

Key points
1. Explore your motivation, overall life situation, and the feelings of loved ones.
2. Avoid impulse decisions. Don't visit pet shelters, pet stores, and other places where pets may be available for sale or adoption if you'll find it hard to resist.
3. When uncertain, give yourself more time.
4. There exists no magic formula but if you heed the above points you will know when the time is right.

Chapter 13

Consulting a Therapist

"Since my cat died I've wanted to be with her so badly that I considered taking all my sleeping pills at once."

"My sister's waiting for me in the car. She drove up from Florida after my rabbit died. She's going to stay with me until I stop feeling suicidal."

"I dragged myself out of the house to get here tonight. I took my first shower in three weeks because I thought you'd throw me out if I showed up as the mess I've been recently. I've missed work, haven't eaten much of anything, and been crying almost nonstop since my parrot died."

When people say such things, Nancy and I know they need more help than the group alone can provide and we strongly encourage a private consultation with a therapist. If you feel this much emotional pain, so much that you consider harming yourself or cannot manage the basics of daily life—you can't get out of bed, feed yourself, or take care of your children, for example—please seek help from a behavioral health professional.

Our recommendation on this point gets even stronger if you find no relief from this level of despair for two weeks or more. This depth and duration of suffering marks the difference between normal grief and clinical depression. Let me repeat this important point: If you consider harming yourself or another person, cannot keep up with the basics of daily life, or feel unrelenting emotional pain for two weeks or longer, then you meet the baseline criteria for a diagnosis of clinical depression and deserve the benefit of a full evaluation.

I use the word "deserve" because many people may feel badly when they get a recommendation for this kind of help. They may feel that they've failed or are showing signs of weakness. If you fall within this group, please ask yourself: Don't we all deserve to enjoy our best possible health? Doesn't everybody deserve care when their health falters?

Treatment for depression, which usually includes talking therapy in combination with prescribed medication, has proven highly effective. No convincing argument can be made for declining this help.

While most people who experience normal grief do not choose to see a therapist and they do fine, even those who do not experience the extremes described above may benefit from speaking with a psychotherapist. Talking with a therapist can bring helpful insights, suggestions you wouldn't gain otherwise, and much support. A therapist can help you get through life's major challenges and the loss of a pet surely qualifies.

Please bear in mind, however, one important caveat. Behavioral health therapists, like all other human beings, hold biases. Some understand well the impact of pet loss. Others, unfamiliar with the normal grieving that follows the loss of a companion animal, may misunderstand your reaction. Some may even mistakenly diagnose your normal grief as emotional illness.

Every one of us deserves the finest assistance available. When seeking a therapist, therefore, it makes sense to go about the search with care. Keep in mind that you offer the therapist a special opportunity. You will invite him or her to help you with your grief, a matter of great personal importance.

If possible, start with recommendations from people who you trust. If you work for a company that offers an employee assistance program (EAP), one of your trusted advisors may be an EAP counseling professional. Your EAP counselor can refer you to local therapists who they know have helped people in similar circumstances.

Consider scheduling interviews with two or more therapists before committing to a series of meetings with any one of them. During these interviews, ask the therapists to describe their experiences helping people who've lost pets. Ask them to describe their overall approach to helping people with the other challenges they bring. Ask *whatever questions* you'd like answered about their professional background and the services they provide. The professional you choose will expect you to share extraordinarily personal matters at a uniquely vulnerable time in your life. It's only reasonable that they share freely with you the details of their professional background and approach to helping.

Because research shows that the quality of the relationship between a therapy client and his or her therapist best predicts the effectiveness of their work together, it makes sense to pay special attention to the way you feel toward those you interview. You will likely achieve your best results with a therapist with whom you feel comfortable and who inspires confidence in their ability to help.

Nancy and I can assure you from personal experience, both as providers and recipients of behavioral health care, of the value in psychotherapy. We can tell you also, as therapists who have logged many years in the field and as trainers of therapists, that our colleagues run the gamut present within all professions: some perform brilliantly, most perform admirably, and a few perform dismally. You owe it to yourself to choose your therapist carefully.

Normal grief, while at times agonizing, doesn't threaten our lives or livelihoods. While consulting with a behavioral health therapist can never hurt, most grief does not require it. Many people who lose pets do not consult with therapists and they find themselves none the worse off as a result. However, if you face destructive impulses or functional collapse as described earlier in this chapter, you face a special kind of grief, one that brings extraordinary suffering and even a degree of personal danger. Please see a behavioral health clinician for a full evaluation, and follow their recommendations. Remember that doing so does not mark you as a failure, a weakling, or a crazy person. On the contrary, your decision to seek professional assistance distinguishes you as a person with good judgment. After all, isn't the willingness to seek help when we need it one of life's most important skills?

Key points
1. Consult with a therapist if your grief immobilizes you for more than two weeks or leads you to self-destructive thoughts and impulses.
2. Depression can be treated very effectively.
3. A therapist can help with normal grief.
4. Choose your therapist (and any helping professional) with care.

Chapter 14

Welcoming Joy Back into Your Life

We've heard from many people that moments of joy make them feel guilty. That may sound strange, so let me explain further. Many people yearn for joyful moments to relieve the unrelenting sadness that has taken over their lives after a pet's death. Then, however, when a happy moment shines through, they feel guilty.

"How can I feel happy at a time like this? What a terrible person I am!"

A backlash of guilt follows each moment of joy.

Watch for this pattern and resist it. Fortify yourself with the certainty that positive feelings never betray your friend's memory. On the contrary, they honor the joyful relationship that you shared with your pet.

What would your departed friend want?

It can help to try the following exercise. Imagine that your deceased pet has the ability to watch your actions, thoughts, and feelings. He or she sees you experience a moment of joy, maybe as you pet your neighbor's new puppy. Then, as soon as you recognize the feeling, you collapse into guilt, calling yourself heartless and self-centered.

How would your friend feel? What would he or she want for you?

The answer may be obvious. Your friend would want you to feel happy. He or she would feel glad witnessing your moment of joy and then saddened as you turned away from it.

This would hold true even if your happiness came as a result of something made possible by your pet's absence, such as an evening out with friends, an extended vacation spent traveling, or welcoming a new pet into your home. Your friend's wish for your happiness would not be soured by jealousy or bitterness. Love doesn't work that way. He or she would want you to welcome every bit of happiness. Your friend would send you the words I echo here: *Joy is never wrong*.

Key points

1. Sometimes you may feel guilty after experiencing joy.
2. Get ready to reassure yourself that your happiness never means any disregard for your pet's memory. It doesn't mean you loved them any less.
3. It can help to ask yourself what your deceased friend would want for you.
4. Welcoming joy never betrays your friend's memory.

Chapter 15

Holding Onto the Lessons of Grief

Put off reading this chapter for a while if your grief feels terribly raw. We'll talk here about the ways that grief changes us and the lessons you can learn as a result. We say "can learn" because many people don't pay attention and, as a result, disregard what could have been life-changing knowledge. What we share in this chapter may not be entirely new to you. Many people have this knowledge, but they hold it in the back of their minds. They don't put what they learn through grief into words, take it to heart, and use it to shape future actions. Of course, moving from learning into action creates real gains, so that's what we want to help you accomplish. We'll start by challenging a commonly held misconception.

Grief brings you back to normal?

Many people imagine that they'll *recover* from grief in the same way that they recover from illness. They assume that after a bout of grief, people "get back to normal." While this expectation may hold true for the flu, it doesn't fit grief. You can't expect to wake up one morning feeling as you did before your pet died, your grief having broken during the night like a fever. Instead, you will more likely notice that living with the loss gradually becomes easier. One day you'll remember your friend and feel a bit sad while also recalling things about them that make you smile, maybe the fun they had playing outdoors, the endearing way that they snored or purred, or how they loved to be scratched behind their ears. Your grief won't have disappeared. Instead, it will have softened.

As the pain of grief changes, you will change as well. You will gain hard-won lessons about love, compassion, patience, and caring for yourself. You will emerge from your grief in a place different from where you started. Nancy and I want to help you hold onto all that you gain. The following sections highlight some of grief's lessons and share suggestions for keeping those lessons alive.

Value love above all else

The old saying "you don't know what you've got until it's gone" captures the most important lesson that grief offers. Somewhere in our gut we've always known this, but the grief we suffer after a significant loss makes the lesson excruciatingly real. In our despair, we feel more deeply than at any other time how much we value the love we share with those most dear to us. We would trade almost anything for a few moments with our lost friend.

If only you can hold this lesson in your heart always. If only you can prevent the complex demands of daily life from getting in the way from now on. Nancy and I know people who resolve to do just that. While they may choose slightly different methods, forming a habit seems the key to success.

A woman told Nancy that every morning she spends a few minutes speaking aloud to her reflection in the bathroom mirror the names of people and animal friends who she loves. She decides what actions she'll take that day to show her love to one or more of those named. At the end of the day she reminds herself, again speaking in front of her bathroom mirror, of how well she followed through and how it felt to do so.

I know a man who writes in his daily calendar the names of two people for whom he's going to do something loving. He checks their names off after taking action and makes sure to savor the feelings that result. He recently told me, "Sometimes these are really simple things, like hugging my cat, scratching under her chin and telling her how much I love her. Sometimes I make a point to send an email to a friend who I haven't heard from in a while sharing how much they mean to me. It feels wonderful to do these things and then reflect on them."

Many of us, me included, sometimes take those we love for granted. Grief challenges us to fight this complacency. If you take this lesson to heart you will make demonstrating love for others a priority every day.

Keep things in perspective

Grief doesn't just emphasize the absolute priority of loving relationships, but it also puts everything else into perspective as well, including difficulties at work, fender-benders, minor disagreements with family members, and other annoyances. All of these become small in significance when we're grieving. Most of us would agree that they should stay that way all the time. Without any pun intended, grief teaches the difference between a matter of life and death and the small stuff. Unfortunately, it's not easy to keep this perspective going as our grief diminishes. In today's fast-paced, stress-filled world, people often blow even small mishaps out of proportion and become needlessly upset.

When you start getting upset, the following questions can help restore perspective: Will it matter in two weeks? Will it make any difference six months from now? Will you even remember it a year from now? Grief provides a lesson in the real priorities. Keeping what you've learned in mind will always serve you well.

Recognize the strength behind compassion and forgiveness

Because a pet depends upon us for their every need, their death almost always leaves us feeling some degree of guilt. Many of us find it hard to offer ourselves compassion and forgiveness. It takes strength to accept that we had no control at all or very limited control over the course of our pet's illness, or the fact that they grew old, or the accident that claimed their life. If you made an error that actually contributed to your friend's death, remember that it takes perhaps even more strength to accept that you are not perfect, that human beings make mistakes that sometimes bring significant consequences despite our best intentions. Grief teaches that compassion and forgiveness toward ourselves and others makes sense because we live in an unpredictable world over which we have limited control.

This lesson, if you find the strength to heed it, can shift the way you approach much in life, including conflicts with other people. You may learn the value in extending the benefit of the doubt, presuming that people try their best, and responding first with compassion and forgiveness rather than contempt. This lesson teaches us to practice kindness.

Alexander Pope's often-cited quotation, "To err is human, to forgive divine," applies here. Keeping a small sign with this message or a similar one emblazoned on it in your car, on your desk at work, or on your refrigerator can help keep this lesson alive as the sting of grief subsides.

Practice patience

If asked by someone who recently lost their pet how long their grief will likely last, you will never go wrong answering "too long." Grief delivers an unsolicited lesson in patience. We tolerate as best we can the shock, confusion, memory lapses, sleep problems, repetition of irresolvable questions, and overall uncertainty that follow the loss of our pet, all the while wishing the ups and downs to end immediately. While nobody likes this lesson, grief can teach us to practice a new relationship with time and expectation. Gradually, we perceive degrees of relief. We experience time's seemingly magical power to calm the pain of loss. Eventually, we come to believe the old saying "this too shall pass."

Patience begins with recognizing the difference between what you can and cannot control. The lesson deepens when you decide to take action only in areas where you have some measure of control and give up trying to change those things over which you have no control. Those familiar with *The Serenity Prayer* know this message and it's one that can benefit us all. On the deepest level, however, patience teaches us to recognize time as our friend.

When you do the best you can to take care of those matters that lie within your control, time will reward you. We hope you decide to carry this lesson forward. If you are highly impatient, as I am, you can enhance your capacity for patience by inviting the support of others whom you love and respect. After you describe want you're striving to achieve, these special people can help you decide upon the actions that you'll take, and they can help you keep expectations realistic. They can encourage you to savor the relief that follows when you let go of things you cannot change and instead focus all of your energy where you have control. They can help you find ways to tolerate your uncertainties and fears during the time it takes to achieve your desired results. They can support you as you practice patience.

Identify your feelings

Grief gives a crash course in emotions. It brings a torrent of feelings with which we must learn to live. Some people already have the necessary skills. Other people, however, have been taught since childhood to shy away in discomfort from strong feelings. For them, there may be much to learn.

Whether you say them out loud, write them down, or just try them out in your head, grief can teach you that it helps to pair feelings with words. Deciding that you feel "longing" for your pet and "despair" over the fact that you'll never see them again gives you at least a small measure of control. Words such as these turn an onslaught of seemingly unmanageable emotional pain into a collection of individually identifiable emotions, each of which can be more easily tolerated. For this reason, assigning words to feelings—frustration, annoyance, disappointment, embarrassment, sadness, confusion, guilt, helplessness, betrayal, happiness, excitement, enthusiasm—is an important life skill.

You can carry this lesson forward by remembering to name what you're feeling whenever you get overloaded or confused. Answering this question in your head, writing down the words that come to mind, and, perhaps best of all, talking things over with a trusted friend, can help you manage your emotions with less distress. This applies when you're struggling through the worst of grief and at all other times as well.

Make every minute count

The loss of a pet forces the realization that each of us has limited time. I don't know about you, but these days my time seems to disappear faster and faster. On top of that, many people, including me, often feel that their time does not belong to them. Nancy and I counsel many people who feel as though life carries them along as if they're stuck on a conveyor belt, have no control over its direction or speed, and see no way to get off. As we've described in other sections of this book, while there will always be many things that lie outside your control, you will make the most of life's opportunities by taking initiative whenever possible.

Several years ago, a friend brought me a stone plaque engraved with the words, "Dream as if you'll live forever, live as if you'll die tomorrow." The plaque stays on my desk as a constant reminder. I try to apply these words by living mindfully and purposefully. By mindfully, I mean striving to stay grounded in the present moment, connected to those in my company, and focused on the experience at hand. By purposefully, I mean setting measurable goals, such as completing this book by a certain date, so I can contribute to the world in a manner that feels planned and meaningful.

These tools, mindfulness and goal-setting, help keep me focused and organized. They may work well for you also. Distractions, complications, and alterations in goals arise continuously, of course, but with these practices kept firmly in mind, I am able to return to the present moment and move toward the future with purpose.

Cultivate resilience

Your capacity to weather your pet's death demonstrates your resilience. At first, you may have asked yourself, "How will I ever get through this?" Now, as your grief becomes more bearable, you have the answers. Take a moment to reflect on all the things you did that helped you keep going. Maybe these included spending more time with friends who love and respect you, writing letters to your departed friend and reading them aloud, learning new meditation skills, taking up yoga, or starting a regular walking program. Maybe you began volunteering at a local animal shelter or perhaps you became more involved in your community of faith. Maybe you worked hard at tolerating your feelings of sadness or guilt instead of running away from them through overwork, or shopping too much, or drinking too much alcohol.

Take a moment to recognize the strengths that you've exercised and honed as you've cared for yourself during this difficult time. Resilience, the capacity to tolerate and bounce back from adversity, doesn't just happen. It results from the actions that you take. Count your resilience as both an achievement and important life skill and vow to keep at the practices that got you through to this point.

Grief moves us through a spiral of pain and learning. While nobody would ever want to hold onto the pain, the hard-earned lessons of grief can be among the most valuable gifts that your deceased pet leaves you. Don't cast this learning aside as the unrelenting demands of the world draw your attention. Hold fast to the lessons you've learned about how to live.

Key points

1. Grief lessens over time but you don't recover. Instead, you change, learn, and grow stronger.
2. Grief teaches important lessons about love, perspective, compassion, forgiveness, patience, the language of emotions, time, and resilience.

3. Don't let the pull of everyday demands lead you to disregard these lessons.
4. Holding these lessons in your head and heart will serve you well always.

Chapter 16

Dialog: A Typical Group Session

This final chapter reconstructs a typical pet loss group session. It gives you a "fly on the wall" perspective so you can get a feel for how such meetings work. Also, the dialog addresses some matters that can use more attention or haven't fit within earlier sections of the book.

Look at this as a dramatization rather than an exact transcript. Like elsewhere, the examples shared here reflect real people and their comments, but we've shielded identities by changing details and in some cases drawing more than one true-life story into a composite.

If you can find a pet loss group in your area, please try it out. You have nothing to lose except the feeling that you're all alone with your grief, but a lot to gain. You stand to meet people who will instantly relate to what you're going through. Such depth of understanding coming from a number of people all at once offers great comfort. There's something about the intensity and similarity of experience, as well as the feeling of safety and support, that invites even relatively shy people to speak their hearts and minds. Of course, it's also fine for those who attend to simply listen. The facilitator sets the structure for the discussion, carefully monitors the conversation, and shapes the content and flow, but the gifts that people give to one another, not what the facilitator says, bring the group's greatest healing effects.

Ken Dolan-Del Vecchio & Nancy Saxton-Lopez

Dialog

Here's what you may hear at one of my sessions:

Ken: Welcome, everybody. I'm Ken Dolan-Del Vecchio and I'll be facilitating the meeting this evening. So you know a little bit about me, let me tell you that I'm a family therapist and I also work as vice president, Health and Wellness, at a multinational corporation, where I'm responsible for the employee assistance program and other services related to behavioral and organizational health. I've been facilitating meetings here for over ten years, and I've had pets as members of my family all my life. Right now I've got three dogs, two rabbits, and three chickens.

We hold this meeting every first and third Tuesday of the month from 7:30 p.m. to 9 p.m. I'm the facilitator on the third Tuesday and my colleague, Nancy Saxton-Lopez, is here on the first Tuesday. Nancy originated the pet loss program here in 1990 and the groups have run steadily since that time.

We'll get started now even though there may be others joining us. As you'll see, the structure for this meeting is pretty open. Sometimes people come from a great distance or they've got scheduling challenges that make it so they need to arrive late or leave a bit early. Nancy and I understand that. Also, please feel free to attend in any sequence that you find helpful. Some people attend every group for several months or even longer. Some people attend a couple of times in a row and then once a month or so from there. Whatever works for you works for us, too.

We hold this meeting because often there's not enough support for people when they experience loss. There often isn't much support when the loss involves another human being and there's usually even less understanding coming our way when we lose a pet. This group brings together people who are dealing with the loss of a pet. People come to the group because an animal companion has recently died or because they face the likelihood that their pet will soon die. Sometimes people come because they want to talk through their options and concerns regarding euthanasia. People sometimes come to the group because their pet was lost or stolen. Sometimes people come not because a pet has died recently or will likely die soon, but because their sadness over a loss that happened some time ago has come back very strongly and they'd like some help. The group offers an opportunity for you to share support, ask and answer questions, learn how others are getting through their difficult time, and gain comfort knowing you're not alone.

I'm going to go around the room and say everybody's name so you'll have a start at remembering and calling each other by name. If we've just met and I get your name wrong, please correct me. I can be bad with names. Also, everybody here knows that even if you don't have trouble remembering names the way I do, grief messes with your short-term memory. So if you forgot the name of another person here tonight, just ask. I guarantee they'll be okay with that. So we have Geoff, Maureen, Alice, and Sharon, who have been here at least a few times before, and Carl, Suzanne, and Paulette, who are joining for the first time today.

Maybe one of the people who've been here before can get us started by giving an update on how you're doing. It will help if you start off by reviewing for the new people the experience that brought you to the meeting in the first place and also mention how long you've been attending.

Geoff: Well I'll get the ball rolling. I'm Geoff and I came to the group for a little more than a year, ending about a year ago, after my cat, Bosley, died. Now I'm back here for the past couple of months because my other cat, Cheshire, who's sixteen years old, has no kidney function left. (Geoff tears up and blows his nose.) The vet says he's probably not in much if any pain, but he's declining fast these last few days—not eating, really sluggish, and limp like a rag doll. It's something the way I'm grieving for him already even though he's not gone yet. I wonder if that will make it easier when he actually goes.

Paulette: I'm so sorry you're going through such a rough time, Geoff. I hate to say this, but when my Mattie, our little schnauzer, died two weeks ago, I'd been bracing for it for months. He had been diagnosed with cancer six months before, and toward the end it was obvious that he was dying. I thought I had come to terms with the fact that we were losing him, but then when he actually died I felt like I got hit with a ton of bricks.

Ken: What you're both talking about is important. When you learn that your pet is dying, that's an enormous loss. You've lost the expectation that he or she will be with you for years to come. Then when your pet actually dies, you've got a whole new loss to grieve. Some people call the first part "anticipatory grief" because you're grieving as a result of anticipating your pet's death. Then you get hit by the grief that follows your pet's actual death. It's possible that the second layer of grief may be a little less severe than it would have been if your pet had died without warning, but there's no way of knowing for sure. The same thing happens when you learn that a human family member has been diagnosed with a terminal illness, like Alzheimer's or end stage cancer.

Paulette: I agree with you. It would be hard to imagine feeling worse than I do right now. I guess if Mattie had died without any warning, it's possible that I'd feel worse, but I can't even imagine what "worse" would feel like.

Geoff: I guess it's hard when you learn that you're going to lose your friend and then it's even harder when you actually do lose them. I can tell you all, though, that just being able to talk about it and hear about how other people are doing—that's been incredibly helpful.

Carl: I feel a little guilty saying this, but I think just knowing what really happened to my dog, even if I learned that she's dead, would feel better than what I've got now. I had a beautiful little five-year-old mutt named Boomerang. I came home one day to find that the front door of my townhouse was unlocked and she was gone. Nothing else seemed to be wrong or missing, just Boomerang wasn't there. I still have no idea what happened. I called the police and they took a report, I've called all the shelters in this part of the state and there's no sign of her, and none of the neighbors saw anything out of the ordinary.

Alice: Oh, wow. A long time ago we had a parakeet that we let have the run of our apartment when we were cleaning his cage and one day we left a window open without thinking and he flew away. There's almost nothing worse than the kind of uncertainty and guilt that comes after something like that.

Sharon: My son and his family went on a camping trip a few years back. They brought their beautiful little golden retriever puppy with them. Somehow he got away from them and ran into the woods. They never found him. I don't think I've ever seen my son so upset. It's so difficult when you just don't know. He kept talking about all the grisly possibilities: cougars, bears, starvation.

Ken: Sharon and Alice, thanks for mentioning those things that happened some time back. I think the points you're making about uncertainty are key for you and for Carl. There's almost nothing worse than not knowing.

Carl: That's for sure. I just can't put all of my "what ifs" aside. If I knew what happened to her at least I'd be able to hold onto that fact, even if it's really sad or upsetting. Not knowing seems like the worst thing possible.

Ken: How do you all think grief progresses differently when there are so many "what ifs?"

Sharon: I just think it makes the whole thing harder. I know my son and his family were devastated by the loss of their puppy. It seems like the hurt eventually got duller, though, as it does eventually with all losses I suppose.

Alice: How much can you beat yourself up and for how long? Eventually, we just got tired of feeling guilty about leaving that window open. We also made up a story that helped us live with what happened. We told one another, my husband and me, that Pancho—that was our parakeet's name—made it all the way to Mexico and was having a great time. We know that's probably not true, but it sort of made it easier.

103

Maureen: It seems like it's just hard no matter how they go. While you were talking about not knowing exactly what happened I was wondering whether I'd rather have seen Jewel— that was my Chow who died four months ago—go through the ordeal that he went through when he got bloat or have had him just disappear. All of a sudden he was in agony, screaming and moaning and paddling while he lay on the floor. We tried to get him into the car and we couldn't move him because when we touched him, he must have hurt so badly that he tried to bite us. He was out of his mind with pain. Eventually, the vet was able to get to our house but by then he was too far gone and was close to death. It turns out that the bloat led to a heart attack. It was so horrible. It's really hard to get the scene out of my mind. As you were talking a little while ago, I was wondering if we would have been better off if he disappeared and we didn't know what happened. The answer I come up with is that it's really hard no matter how you lose a loved one. It's just really, really, really hard!

Carl: Maureen, that sounds like something out of a night-mare. These stories do kind of put Boomerang's disappearance in a little bit of a different perspective. I believe what you're all saying about the pain getting a little bit duller over time. It's like every day I go over the same questions, but they do get just a little bit older and more familiar, like what Sharon and Alice talked about. I guess I can imagine maybe someday just getting worn out by them and not wanting to ask them so much.

Ken: One of the ways I have come to understand grief is that you take a loss, like Boomerang's disappearance or Chesire's impending death or Jewel's sudden agonizing death, and you emo-tionally "chew" on it. You ask yourself the what-ifs, why-didn't-Is, why-didn't-the-vet; you go over the would-haves, should-haves, and could-haves; you revisit what you saw and heard and felt, until you just can't do it anymore. You chew on this stuff alone and you chew on it with the help of those whom you love and trust with your grief. You keep doing it until that horribly sad, sharply painful news becomes duller, achey, older news. Your ability to pay such intense attention to it wears down and as a result you start paying more pay attention to other things.

(Many group members nod in agreement.)

Maureen: Sometimes I wonder if people like me and my husband grieve much more strongly when our pets die than people who have children. Our dogs basically become our kids, and I wonder if that's made us a little kooky when it comes to dealing with their deaths.

Geoff: I've wondered the same thing. I've told my parents that my cats are basically my children in order to give them some idea of how much they mean to me. I don't have any human children.

Ken: Well, who else, in addition to me, has kids? I've give you my thoughts, but I'm wondering who else wants to respond first.

Paulette: I've got two grown children. When they were both in grammar school our first schnauzer, Sigmund, died. I was so grief-stricken that every day for a while I had to remind myself to give enough attention to the kids. The love I feel for my dogs is similar to what I feel for my kids but it's also different. I have to say that while I'm devastated by the grief I feel for my dogs, I can't compare that to what I'd experience if, God forbid, I faced the loss of one of my kids. That would be grief on a different level.

Sharon: There's no comparison for me. Losing one of my children would feel like the end of my world. Losing one of my pets, on the other hand, feels like the end of an era. I expect my pets to die because their life spans are so short compared to ours. I love them a lot, but there's a huge difference between that kind of loss and what the loss of a child would feel like.

Ken: I agree. I'm grief-stricken when one of my pets dies. Honestly, though, I can't even think about the possibility of losing my child without my stomach going into knots. Years of experience tell me that, in general, parents often get as distressed by the loss of their pets as non-parents. Grief over a lost pet can be devastatingly severe in both instances. Still, the grief most parents would go through were they to suffer the loss of their child would likely feel far more severe than what they experience when a pet dies.

Geoff, I like that you tell your parents to think of your cats as your children because I think the comparison helps them imagine the way you feel. For parents and non-parents who don't connect emotionally with companion animals, comparing your pets to children gives them an analogy to work from. Of course in doing so you presume that they relate to children in a way that's as full of love and concern as the way you relate to your pet. From what we know about parenting, however, that unfortunately may be quite a presumption.

Suzanne: I've got what may be a strange question. Ever since my cat, Jerry, died three weeks ago, my dog, Jagger, has been in a funk. At first I thought he was feeling sad because I've been feeling sad, but I keep seeing him with his head resting on the window sill where Jerry used to spend a lot of time and he just looks so forlorn. Do you think he's grieving for Jerry too?

Geoff: I'm sure of it. (Many others nod their heads in agreement.) When Bosley died, Chesire was inconsolable. He didn't eat very well, he had very little energy, and he just looked sad. I know, you're thinking, "How can a cat look sad? This guy is nuts."

Sharon: No we're not. We know exactly what you mean! (Everybody nods.)

Geoff: Okay, I guess I forgot who I was talking to. (Laughs.)

Paulette: We have another schnauzer, Gilligan, and he seems oblivious to Mattie's death. If anything, I think he's happy that now he doesn't have to share us with another dog. But we've had other dogs and cats who seemed devastated when they lost one of their animal housemates. I think the degree to which pets take notice of deaths in the family varies.

Ken: I agree. Sometimes pets seem to grieve and sometimes they don't seem to be moved by the loss. What have you done to help pets get through their grief?

Alice: Well, my rabbit, Fluffster, seemed pretty upset after his sister, Pom-Pom, died three months ago. I just made a point to give him some extra attention and that seemed to help.

(Others nod in agreement.)

Sharon: We do the same thing. We give our surviving pets some extra TLC and that seems to go a long way toward helping them feel better.

Geoff: I just made sure to give Cheshire lots of extra hugs. I figured that he and I were feeling pretty much the same way about losing Bosley.

Suzanne: That's what I've been doing. I make a point to pet Jagger and say, "I know, I miss him too," when I find him at that window sill. He doesn't usually move except to shift his eyes and look at me. He definitely gets that we're in this together.

Afterward

After a group ends, a feeling of calm settles over me, softening the watchfulness with which I followed the meeting's progress. As I say goodbye to those who attended, I have the opportunity to relax and begin reflecting upon what I'll take away from the meeting.

Preparing to leave, a man stands, then jabs his hands into his pockets searching for car keys. After finding them, he shakes my hand, thanks me, and heads out the door. After most of the rest have said goodbye and left the room, a young woman slowly pulls on her woolen coat and swishes her hair so it all falls outside her collar. She blows her nose into a tissue one last time, and then gathers her purse and the hemp bag that holds the photo album she passed around the room. She reaches out both hands to clasp mine. With eyes open wide and lips pressed into a brave smile, she whispers, "Thank you," and leaves.

Alone now, I scan for items left behind and find none. As I shut the lights I sense movement in the room, vibrations in the ether as light becomes dark. How could it be otherwise in a place so recently overflowing with the longing for departed souls?

On the walkway that leads to the parking lot I pass two people sharing some last thoughts. A group of three also lingers, speaking softly. We wave to one another as I pass. Leaving here brings completion as well as continuity. Much has been shared and the healing will continue through more of the same.

I never feel alone on my ten-minute drive home. Having spent such a time with these people, it's almost as though they ride along with me. Their words repeat in my thoughts, messages of love and pain that make me consider my own pets and what they mean to me. I think of Jack, Abigail, and Isabel, the little dogs who will greet me excitedly when I open the front door a few moments from now. I'll pat their fuzzy, warm heads and tickle behind their pointed ears. Our touch will bring me a renewed sense of appreciation. All that happened in the meeting highlights the preciousness of these friends and the brevity of our time together. And I think of Reggie, Phoebe, Lily, and my other departed pets. The people with whom I shared the evening demonstrated for me once again the miracle of grief, for there was a time following the loss of each of these pets when thoughts of them would bring only searing pain. I reflect on how grief eventually turns heartache into gratitude.

Having written these words, my thoughts turn to you. I wish I could spare you the pain, confusion, anger, and weariness that stand between now and that future moment when the pain of your grief has lessened. But wishing won't change forces beyond human control. So, I hope that these pages have given you ideas and suggestions to help you through the time ahead.

Nancy and I have been asked many times if the worst pain of grief will ever end. We can answer with certainty that it will. One day you will recall your lost pet and smile. Your grief, which may still feel raw as you read these words, will eventually lead you to that moment. Your pain will grow ever smaller, but the love you feel for your pet will be yours to keep.

Acknowledgements

Ken's Gratitude

Nancy Saxton-Lopez invited me into the work of helping people with the loss of their animal companions. I will always be grateful for the opportunity and her collaboration on this book.

I thank Ed Sayres for believing in our project and lending his support.

I thank Heather Cammisa, Nora Parker, and the rest of the team at St. Hubert's Animal Welfare Center for supporting our pet loss groups all these years, and for everything else they do for animals and their companion people.

My family therapy mentor and friend, Monica McGoldrick, taught me to see the big picture, how we are each shaped by family, community, culture, and history. I thank her for sharing her wisdom with such generosity and her support on this and my other writing projects.

I thank Lynn Parker for her enthusiastic support for the book. While she lives at a distance, Lynn is never far from my thoughts. I am so fortunate to have her as a friend.

A veterinarian, Tony Miele, regularly witnesses the pain that comes with the loss of a pet. I am grateful for his endorsement of our book as a helpful resource.

Many thanks go to Celinda English, a brilliant artist and fashion designer who loves animals (and me) enough to have crafted several pieces of art as suggestions for the book's cover.

Time and again, Cyndie Fearon proves that a friend in need is a friend indeed. A PowerPoint and Photoshop virtuoso, Cyndie, made several images that helped us design the cover.

My friend, Rick Keshishian, encouraged this project before a word was written, never failing to list *The Pet Loss Companion* on the agenda of our monthly breakfast summits and ask me what's taking so long. I am grateful for his interest and support.

I thank Rich Rassmann, my colleague and friend. Rich is a skilled editor and journalist whose punctuation and grammatical edits, along with his suggestions on content, sharpened the text.

Shirley Cresci and I work together every day and she still seems to like me. I could not hope for a more skilled or good-natured colleague. I am grateful for her partnership and for her helpful advice on the manuscript.

Other friends and colleagues who I'd like to thank include Andy Crighton, Maureen Corcoran, Sharon Dumont, Myrtho Montes, Mona Rosbury-Yoder, Addy Cruz, Diane Hettinger, Judy Martin, Julie Bukar, Theresa Messineo, Roberto Font, Marie Hitchman, Mariam Banafti, Laura Docherty, Jud Wampole, Suze Albright, Mary Aun, Catherine Lugg, Wesley Curl, Ed and Karin O'Donnell, Jackie Hudak, Sarah Stearns, Nydia Garcia-Preto, Gloria McDonald, Karen Shernan, and Fred Levine. Each helped make the book possible.

I thank my son, Erik, for his compassion toward all living beings and his thoughtful regard for the big questions. His presence in my life, the most important gift I've received, provides endless inspiration.

I thank Lynn Dolan, Erik's mother, my co-parent, and friend. Her strength, grace, humor, and wisdom have benefited me throughout this journey called adulthood.

I thank my parents, Barbara and Joseph Del Vecchio, who modeled humility and kindness toward animals, and have now transitioned into the next cycle. You are forever in my heart. Blessed be.

I thank David Drummond and his partner, Sterling McAndrew, for their friendship and constant encouragement. My life would be much smaller without them.

I thank my animal companions past and present: Pinky, Shaggy, Agrippina, Nero, Melvin, Henry, O'Henry, Reginald, Phoebe, Miss Melissa, Lily, Jack, Isabel, Abigail, Sol, Terra, Lady

Drummond, Henrietta, and Gertrude, each one a beautiful soul who has enriched my life and taught me about the meaning of love and the healing that grief brings.

Finally, I thank my husband, Tim Garrett. Tim teaches me volumes about the magic of words and the magic of love. He is my warmth, heat, and light; my special other person whose creativity, thoughtfulness, and capacity for love exceed and inspire my own.

Nancy's Gratitude

I thank all my best friends and loves: the dogs of my childhood, Patty, Princess, Sandy, Cocoa Bean, Peter, Paul, Skippy, Brick, Blackie and Spooky; and the pug dogs of my adult years who just didn't live long enough, Tashi (The First Lady), Noelle (The Grand Dame), LuLu (My Homegirl), and Fred (My Son); also, to my nephew, Bear, and special niece, Maggie; the cockatiels, Tweety, Henry I, and Henry II, and my rescue mouse, Larry.

I especially want to thank Ed Sayres, who in 1989 was President and CEO of St. Hubert's Giralda in Madison, New Jersey. He, Meg Struble (thank you so much!), and Nora Parker (thank you so much!) provided essential support—a location, advertising and hands-on involvement—that moved the pet loss group concept to reality. Without them, I'm not sure the group would have survived to become one of the longest-running companion animal loss support groups in the State of New Jersey.

I thank Heather Cammisa and the rest of the staff at St. Hubert's for their ongoing support.

I also want to thank the Reverend Carolyn Carpenter, who started the group with me in 1990 and was my partner in providing companion animal loss counseling and support for 12 years. The marriage between clinical and spiritual was very helpful to those who attended. I still refer to Carolyn's spiritual sayings.

I thank Ken for inviting me to be part of the writing of this book. It has been wonderful collaborating with him and sharing the

Ken Dolan-Del Vecchio & Nancy Saxton-Lopez

leadership of the Companion Animal Loss Support Group for over 11 years. You are a kindred spirit.

I thank Tony Miele, DVM, for his support throughout the years and offering so quickly to read our manuscript and give us an endorsement. He was one of the first veterinarians I met who believed in the importance of the human animal bond. He gave me an opportunity to speak to his practice in Brooklyn about companion animal loss in the early 1990's.

And Tim (Ken's husband), you are certainly a very creative guy! Thanks for the beautiful cover!

Thanks also to my husband, Peter, who shares my love of pugs, and my daughter, Elisa (my everlasting light), who loves the pugs more than she admits (especially Molly).

Many thanks to my cousin Barbara, who shares our family experience and always is a comforting support.

And last but not least, I thank Gina (for ALWAYS being there), Kristen (who understands so well the human animal bond because she was the Best Mom to Maggie), and Branka. These three special friends have given me over twenty-five years of love and support.

About the Authors

Ken Dolan-Del Vecchio is a Licensed Marriage and Family Therapist (LMFT) and Licensed Clinical Social Worker (LCSW) who has led monthly pet loss groups for eleven years. He is a life-long animal companion enthusiast, having shared his home with dogs, cats, chickens, rabbits, cockatiels, finches, chinchillas, guinea pigs, turtles, mice, one horse, and one rat. A special rat, indeed, Nero sat on Ken's shoulder eating peanuts while Ken studied late into the evenings at college. Ken earned his B.A. in biopsychology at Cornell University and Master of Social Work (MSW) at Hunter College of the City University of New York. He completed a three year post-graduate program in family therapy at The Multicultural Family Institute, Highland Park, New Jersey, where he now serves on the board of directors. Ken makes his living as a health and wellness executive at a multinational company. He is a father and husband who lives with his family in Palmer, Massachusetts, and

Newark, New Jersey. Ken is the author/coauthor of two previous books, *Making Love, Playing Power: Men, Women and the Rewards of Intimate Justice* and *Transformative Family Therapy: Just Families in a Just Society.*

Nancy Saxton-Lopez is a Licensed Clinical Social Worker (LCSW), Diplomate in Clinical Social Work (DCSW), and psychotherapist who began the Companion Animal Loss Support Group at St. Hubert's Giralda in Madison New Jersey, on April 3, 1990. Nancy earned her Master of Social Work (MSW) at New York University. She received a Certificate in Family Therapy from the Center of Family Studies in Springfield, New Jersey. Currently, Nancy is a Senior Partner in a behavioral healthcare consulting firm and has a private practice. She loves all animals and has shared her home with many dogs, birds, fish and a mouse. She lives with her daughter, husband, and four black pugs in Ridgewood, New Jersey.

Additional Resources

Websites:

www.aplb.org(Association of Pet Loss and Bereavement)
www.petloss.com
www.pet-loss.net
www.aspca.org.
www.rainbowbridge.com
www.hoofbeats-in-heaven.com
www.argusinstitute.colostate.edu
www.facebook.com/petloss
www.mypetloss.com
www.deltasociety.org
www.humanesociety.org
(and many more – just enter "pet loss" in your browser)

Every Veterinary Medicine School has a pet loss page.
The top five (from *US News and World Report*):
Cornell, New York
UC Davis, California
Colorado State University, Colorado
University of North Carolina, North Carolina
Ohio State, Ohio
University of Pennsylvania, Pennsylvania

Ken Dolan-Del Vecchio & Nancy Saxton-Lopez

Books:

> *Coping with Sorrow on the Loss of Your Pet*, Moira Anderson Allen
> *The Loss of a Pet,* Wallace Sife
> *Pet Loss: A Thoughtful Guide for Adults and Children*, Herbert Nieburg and Arlene Fischer
> *Going Home: Finding Peace When your Pets Die*, Jon Katz
> *Dog Heaven,* Cynthia Rylant
> *Cat Heaven*, Cynthia Rylant
> *Goodbye Friend: Healing Wisdom for Anyone Who Has Ever Lost a Pet*, Gary Kowalski
> *For Every Dog an Angel*, Christine Davis
> *For Every Cat an Angel*, Christine Davis
> *When Your Pet Dies, A Guide to Mourning, Remembering and Healing,* Alan Wolfelt
> (and many more; ask your librarian or go on book websites such as Amazon and Barnes and Noble)

62745486R00076

Made in the USA
Lexington, KY
17 April 2017